# THE BACK HOME SERIES

Praise for
# Robert Miltner

## *Ohio Apertures*

"Ohio's true beauty is the trick of its commonness. With its gray-brown birds, flyover skies, and the smallest of the Great Lakes, it fools one into thinking it unworthy of note. Then along comes a poet canny enough to summon its charms. In *Ohio Apertures*, Robert Miltner mines his homegrown memories and vernacular landscapes, reanimating lakeside taverns and riverbank afternoons, Wonder bread and tater tots, the Indians on the radio and the Eagles on the jukebox. With warmth and lyrical ease, these essays and reflections grant dignity to the commonplace."

—David Giffels, *The Hard Way on Purpose: Essays and Dispatches from the Rust Belt* and *Barnstorming Ohio: To Understand America*

"Following the advice of James Thurber to 'look around with awareness,' Robert Miltner's *Ohio Apertures* is an album of perfectly-focused poetic takes on his remembered and actual Ohio. A native of the North Shore, he describes his boyhood in Cleveland and then Avon Lake, and his academic peregrinations elsewhere in the state. Along the way, his brief but fully satisfying narratives celebrate the birds, trees, and rivers of his part of Ohio, as well as his own family and heirlooms, and their long connections to the past. Wonderfully, as he reminisces about his grandmother's home-baked bread, he bursts into a paean to the croissant.

Writing in *The Long-Legged House*, Wendell Berry warns, 'a man can be provincial only by being blind and deaf to his province.' *Ohio Apertures* is a notable response. Robert Miltner has followed his sentences to places sharply remembered, brilliantly rendered, and wisely understood."

—Richard Hague, *Earnest Occupations: Teaching, Writing, Gardening, and Other Local Work*

"Exploration, discovery, and a sense of wonder animate these tightly crafted lyric memoirs. Whether a memory is recounted from the adolescent or adult looking-back perspective, the writer's lens deftly pans backdrop, then zooms in to capture key details; his aperture fully open and focused. The writing shimmers on the continuum between poetry and prose: powered by the engines of both narrative and that of rhythmic language and imagery. Situated squarely in space and time—Cleveland in the '50s—these pieces are small marvels of shared adventure. The reader is drawn into each scene, each revelation, engaged by Miltner's flowing speech lines. In this collection, the writer clearly communicates his 'ability to remain astonished' while astonishing the reader with personal history and insights. *Ohio Apertures* represents storytelling at its lyric best."

—Barbara Sabol, *Solitary Spin* and *Imagine a Town*

"When I think of poetry that moves me, Robert Miltner's poetry is what I think of, and *Ohio Apertures*, his first book of creative non-fiction, is as poetic as anything he's written. Miltner softens the line between prose and poetry, and his skillful non-fiction acts as escort through the Ohio of his youth and beyond. With flawless language, this book does two things: As it reaches deep into the author's past, it artfully widens the aperture for me to reach into my own childhood, my own lost youth."

—Bob Kunzinger, *The Iron Scar* and *A Third Place: Notes in Nature*

"*Ohio Apertures* is a volume aglow with specifics: a Datsun B-210, an orphaned diamond cufflink, the color of the sky over Lake Erie. Miltner's gorgeous essays are rooted in a life lived locally but never provincially—confirming again and again that Ohio is itself the world and that 'what was under the surface of the Jordan River was also what was under the surface of the Rock River.'"

—Angela Sorby, *Bird Skin Coat* and *The Sleeve Waves*

# Ohio Apertures

*A Lyric Memoir by*

Robert Miltner

Cornerstone Press
*Stevens Point, Wisconsin*

Cornerstone Press, Stevens Point, Wisconsin 54481
Copyright © 2021 Robert Miltner
www.uwsp.edu/cornerstone

Printed in the United States of America.

Library of Congress Control Number: 2020949659
ISBN: 978-1-7333086-5-6

Cornerstone Press titles are produced in courses and internships offered by the Department of English at the University of Wisconsin–Stevens Point.

DIRECTOR & PUBLISHER     EXECUTIVE EDITOR     DEVELOPMENT COORDINATOR
Dr. Ross K. Tangedal     Jeff Snowbarger      Alexis Neeley

SENIOR PRESS ASSISTANT
Johanna Honoré

PRESS STAFF
Colin Aspinall, Colton Bahr, Shelby Ballweg, Seth Barnes, Kala Buttke, Ryan Condon, Kyra Goedken, Tucker De Guelle, Andrew Eisele, Amber Elsworth, Emma Fisher, Ava Freeman, Morgan Frostman, Sid Hart, Claire Hoenecke, Nichole Hougard, Amy Jordan, Aya Kacprzynski, George Klumb, Jacob Maczuzak, Gavrielle McClung, Kiera Meidenbauer, Dylan Morey, James Paul, Katelyn Pietroske, Abigail Shortell, Tara Sparbel, Katelyn Voorhies

*For Genevieve Alice Higgins Miltner*
*and Eugene Charles Miltner*

Also by Robert Miltner:

FICTION
*And Your Bird Can Sing*

POETRY
*Orpheus & Echo*
*Hotel Utopia*

POETRY CHAPBOOKS
*Against the Simple*
*Queen Mab and the Moon Boy*
*Eurydice Rising*
*Ghost of a Chance*
*Imperative*
*Rock the Boat*
*A Box of Light*

# Contents

# ONE

*Our obsessions are seeded in childhood, and we spend our adult lives seeking out our own versions of what we have learned...*
–Alex Preston

# Double Exposure

July sunshine strikes the indigo surface of the Blue Hole in Castalia, Ohio. The reflection is as brilliant as candle flames seen through a crystal glass, as a table lamp-illuminated bedroom window on a winter's night in northern Ohio, or like light flaring off of the lens of a camera as it captures and holds a moment. A passing cloud apertures the distinct vibrant hue of the bottomless sinkhole. The water reflects as blue as the iris of an eye. Observe the fidgeting boy impatient to get to Sandusky on the pencil-thin sand and rock paved causeway to Cedar Point Amusement Park.

Imagine the boy's held-breath anticipation of the roller coaster as it rises, the paused instant at the top from which he sees for a mile or more. Picture his plummeting down the first hill and the centrifugal lean into the first curve, his shoulder and hip pressed against the side of the car, the seemingly endless ups and downs. Feel the sudden cool darkness of the exit tunnel where the brake grabs, rocking the coaster to a stop.

Autumn leaves float across the green water pond. They could be aluminum fishing boats seen from the corrugated sheet-metal Ford Tri-Motor airplane. The low-flying Tin Goose cruises one of the world's shortest air routes, from Port Clinton to South Bass Island, in the western basin of Lake Erie. Perch and walleye fishermen look up from their bobbers and wave from their boats as the shadow of the old plane crosses over them.

As the plane nears shore, its small windows fill with the faces of ten passengers who raise their squinting eyes into the dark holes of their Canon and Nikon viewfinders. They hold their breath as the pilot tips the left wing to descend and land in a tractor-mowed farm field outside Put-In-Bay where the aircraft bounces and settles.

The passengers land then walk to the road that will lead into town for a day or week of swimming, barhopping, and vineyard tasting revelries. Some will visit Heineman's Winery to descend into the Crystal Cave, the world's largest geode of blue celestite angel stone. As they approach the small Quonset hut hanger that serves as a terminal, one man notices his split-image reflection in a nearby aquamarine pond glinting in the sunshine of early Indian Summer. He pauses a moment, as if posing.

# Shadows of Crows Crossing Over

I am six years old and looking for angels. My lifted face scans the vast gray Ohio sky above the alley behind my Grandma Carrie's house on Cleveland's near west side. A blue jay breaks from a mulberry tree and flaps above the two-story wooden house on West 94th street where my mother grew up. Shadows of mourning doves pass over me. There are no angels to be seen. My grandma has just died.

Inside the house, my mother and the adults are distracted, distraught. My mother cries, as does her sister Ruth and my Aunt Virginia, all three sitting at the kitchen table. Uncle Bob, my mother's brother, and my dad sip whiskey from juice glasses, shake their heads, rest their hands briefly on their wives' shoulders, then drop them to their sides as they lean silently against the counter.

My younger cousin Kathy, my older cousin Tom, and my older brother Dick and I are all sent from the house. We go out through the back gate, a wooden frame stapled with chicken wire, and into the alley. Our parents and grandma rarely come out past the gate, so it's the place we kids will be left alone. Something between a narrow street and a sidewalk lined with garages, alleys seem like a mysterious pathway, like something from a book.

We stand near a blackened barrel used to burn trash. Gathered in a happenstance circle at its base are burned wood fragments, a crushed tin can, dust and debris, soot and ashes. In the alley behind grandma's house, we act as quiet as if we are in church. If we speak at all, we whisper.

At mass on Sundays at Saint Patrick's church I think about angels. Outside, where Puritas Avenue crosses Rocky River Drive, is the small, old stone church cemetery we walk past to enter. Seated inside, I can't read the hymnal or the missal much, so I turn the pages, stopping at the pictures of the Holy Ghost who is sometimes presented as a child's head with small wings where his ears should be, or as a baby Jesus. I'm more interested in the pictures of angels. They look a lot like Jesus, yet they have large wings, and they usually appear kneeling and praying. Once I saw the image of an angel lifting someone up into heaven, holding a haloed saint by the hand as they hovered over weeping women. I kept looking on Sundays for that picture but I never found it again. Now my grandma has died. I imagine a winged angel's hand reaching for my Grandma Carrie. I picture the two of them rising up on an elevator of clouds.

Dick pokes at the ashes in the trash barrel with a stick. Kathy sniffles and cries softly. Tom starts making a small drum sound. He hops to the beat and circles the trash barrel. Dick moves out of his way. Kathy stands staring, her mouth open but not saying anything. "Grandma's dead," Tom chants, "Grandma's dead." Dick and Kathy and I start to follow Tom, circling too, also making drum sounds. Our bodies move erratically, as exaggerated as puppets on strings. I feel a day of pent-up energy igniting. Dancing around the barrel is like a match and I am catching on fire. "Grandma's dead," we chant, growing louder, moving faster.

Tom begins to lift, to rise, to take flight. His face, wide-eyed and open mouthed, is a mask not unlike the faces of martyrs on a holy card, an expression caught between surprise and fright. What suspends him in the air though is not an archangel, a dominion, or throne, but my Uncle Bob, a policeman and decorated war hero, who holds his son, his left arm hooked under Tom's arm pit, his right hand like a vise on the back of his neck. Kathy and Dick and I turn into stone statues, silent and still.

My Uncle Bob's shoes sound sharp on the gravel then dull as he carries Tom through the gate and into the yard. In a fluid motion he lowers and releases Tom, who sprints beyond the reach of his father and toward the house as his feet find traction. I can see the wooden steps of the rear door where my mother is crying, a bunched handkerchief held to her face, leaning against my father, while Aunt Virginia leans against her, wringing her hands. Aunt Ruth stands alone, saying, "Oh, oh, oh," her hands clutched at her neck.

Uncle Bob stops and turns back toward the three of us outside the gate. I expect a sharp, angry look, followed by his usual bellowing, telling us to get in the house. But he doesn't. He just looks sad, his face a sagging, crumpled paper bag, sadder than any adult I've ever seen. Then he nods to us a few times and returns to the steps, the women, the loss.

Dick and Kathy follow him toward the house. They don't look back. From the alley I watch them pass into the house until the back steps are empty, the door closed.

Something has changed, but I'm not sure what. It's like I have pieces to a jigsaw puzzle, though I don't have the finished picture to look at for a model. When we chanted and danced, I sensed the loss of the moment lift, knew an odd exhilaration. Now it seems flat, common. A heavy coat of emptiness weighs upon me.

From above, a raucous noise calls my attention. An erratic trio of crows wing and glide against the gray sky. As they swoop and caw, their dark shadows pass over me. Instinctively I genuflect, yet offer no prayer. Then I run as fast as I can toward the house, flapping my wings as if I've become a bird.

# The Swift Currents of Spring Rivers

It was spring and I was halfway to my sixth birthday. I stood on a grassy bank of the Rocky River that ran through the valley floor of the Cleveland Metroparks. From that natural platform, I could look across the river to the golf course, the horse stables, and the bridle path. The water was deep enough that the stone ford had disappeared from view.

My father had warned me not to go down to the Rocky River on my own. Even at my young age of five I knew by the tone of his voice that he was serious.

A river can be dangerous, he'd told me. If a current catches you, even if you're a strong swimmer, he had said, it won't let go.

Tossing twigs and broken sticks into the river was fun. I liked watching the way the water would catch and whisk the debris quickly down river before making it disappear. As I leaned over to see where the water turned around a bend, the soft riverbank, undercut by spring currents, suddenly gave way.

The river pressed against my mouth, my nostrils, my ears, my eyelids. My feet slipped in the slick mud of the river bottom. My body felt the brisk insistence of the current, like strong arms grasping my ankles, legs. My canvas shoes pulled me down. Water rose over my forehead until I was completely submerged.

I pushed off the rocky bottom with my feet and up through the river surface, like a porpoise seeking air. The weight of my soaked clothing continued to weigh me down. Again I pushed off, up, gasping for air.

Grasping at the nearby bank, an arm's length a way, I clawed at the tall, easytograb grass coming loose in my hands. Finally a tree root held, held its ground on the riverbank, held me. Tree roots, I learned, are more reliable than grass.

I lifted my water-soaked body up out of the river. I shook like a bird fallen from a nest, a minnow on shale, a child who'd been in over his head. Guarded by the leafing greens of May's developing canopy of trees, I lay still, not wanting to return home because I feared getting in trouble. I knew that my parents' disappointment in me would result in a stern lecture, followed by keeping a much closer eye on me. I decided to stay in the woods before leaving the valley. The wind, like a current of air, passed over me until my clothes dried out.

Back at home, I was given dinner and sent upstairs to my room for bedtime. I heard my mother humming a melody. The running tap water sang along as she washed the dinner dishes. I lay awake awaiting sleep, listening as my older brother recited altar boy Latin, discerning the *Introibo ad altare Dei* chant for the pouring of water over the priest's hands during the consecration of the eucharist.

I also overheard Bishop Fulton J. Sheen talking on the television downstairs as my father listened. Sheen's voice ran on about water, about John the Baptist, and the River Jordan, and being saved. But I was young and did not understand the meaning or significance of the difference between the soul and the flesh. The drowsy cadence of Sheen's words washed over me, lulling me. My eyelids grew heavy, and soon I was carried away by the strong current of sleep.

Time passed before I understood that what was under the surface of the Jordan River was also what was under the surface of the Rocky River. The intention of both rivers became clear to me: rivers and their currents can be dangerous. I could have died that day when I fell off the riverbank. I thought I had beaten the river's intent, its insistence, but I had not. The river rejected me, jettisoned me back upon the land—death by drowning was not to be my fate.

That night, years ago, when I closed my eyes in my dormer bedroom, I saw an image of my own ghost swimming in the ripples of the river. And long has that image haunted me. Even now, as I close my eyes, the weight of those water-soaked clothes from the river that baptized me is with me. Still I feel the current's pull.

# A Boy Among Books

I'm allowed to go four places on my own in Avon Lake. One is Saint Joseph's Parish on Lake Road, where I go to school and to church. One is Blesser Field, with its baseball diamond and the ice rink where I skate in the winter. Another is Mayor's Park, with its swings and benches, next to the old Folger house where the Mayor's office is, up on a shale bluff above the sand beach and the small boat marina. The last one is the town's small public library.

I arrive by one-speed bike at the library, on Center Road, next to Miller Creek near the high school and half a mile south of Lake Erie. It's an old two-story house that has been converted into a library by building a flat-roofed porch and adding a room on the back. The house roof is covered in wide horizontal bands of tarpaper that run parallel to the white clapboard siding. The library sits snug against the flat landscape on the north coast of Ohio. Men from New England who settled here cleared the pin oaks and elms to plant apple orchards and Concord grape vineyards that sweetened in the late harvest due to the "lake effect" warm autumn temperature of the lake. In the fall during the football season, on cold, clear nights, the air is thick with the scent of grape jam.

The July morning is warm already and it will be hot by early afternoon. I get off of my bike and push down the kickstand with my right foot. There are three cars parked

13

in the cinder lot. Mine is the only bike, here on the front lawn, near the large evergreen shrubs. I leave my tackle box in the front basket and lay the fishing rod and reel across the handlebars.

I stop and sit on the lowest of the three steps that lead to the porch. The shoelace on my left Converse sneaker is coming loose and I want to make sure it's tight. I untie it, pull the laces, and retie my shoe. I have shorts at home, but I like my dungarees better. My dad told me that he didn't get long pants until he was in high school, so I feel grown up for an eight-and-a-half-year-old boy.

I walk up the three steps to the porch. To the right of the screen door is an aluminum glider under the windows, its green canvas seat looks well-used by people who sit outside, reading or waiting for someone to check out or return books.

A small bell rings once as I open the screen door to enter and rings again as I close it. The librarians can hear someone enter from wherever they are on the first floor. I stand waiting at the oak desk just inside the front room. In my pocket are eight coins, two for each book, each book two days late. I'm bringing back *Billy and Blaze* and *Blaze Finds the Trail*.

Blaze is a smart horse, always helping Billy. I like the way Clarence William Anderson illustrates his books with drawings of horses. I like that he uses his middle name. I wish the pictures were in color.

I wish I had a horse. When I walk through the woods near my house, I get to a farm pasture with a brown horse with a black mane and tail, and a miniature horse colored like a Palomino. I pull grass from my side of the wire fence and hold it out to them. The larger horse comes over and I pet its nose while it takes the stalks of grass from my hands. If I bring apples I've picked from one of the abandoned orchards, the small horse will come for wild Winesaps.

The clock ticks. 10:22. The calendar on the wall says 1957. Warm air from the west comes in through the screen door behind me, and from the south through the screened window to my right. On the desk is a deep wooden tray marked Returns. *The Man in the Gray Flannel Suit. The Town. Peyton Place. Horton Hears a Who. What Johnny Can't Read.* No, that's wrong. *Why Johnny Can't Read.*

The summer library assistant, a high school girl with a ponytail and dark-rimmed glasses, comes out of the back room. She puts the coins I give her for my late fees in a cigar small box that she puts in the desk drawer, then returns to the back room without saying a word to me.

I walk past the desk to the staircase that takes me to the second floor which holds the children's section. The steps are narrow and the walls close. It's dark halfway up. I emerge from the stairs through what was once a trapdoor, into the low-ceilinged, slant-walled half-story of an attic.

Bookshelves line the walls and two back-to-back sets of bookcases run down the center, taking up almost the whole length of the second floor. It's like a long playhouse filled with books. In the winter, because there is no heating duct to the second floor, it is so cold I can almost see my breath.

It's hot up here. Only the north window opens all the way. Because the window ropes are broken, the other window, the south one from which the air is moving, is barely held open with an old scuffed hardback book. It's stuffy and the air is musty with the scent of old paper. I see dust motes in the sunlight. Sweat prickles my temples. I start walking among the books, feeling sweat dampening the back of my neck by the hairline.

The books in the children's section are arranged by how well a child can read. The shelf starts with picture books and early readers. *Fun With Dick and Jane. Lassie and Her Day in the Sun. The Cat in the Hat.* I move on to the illustrated books where I stop and look for *Blaze and the Gypsies.* It must still be checked out. I'll look again next time. *The Lone Ranger and the Ghost Horse. First Book of Space Travel. Molly the Rogue. Freddy the Pig and the Baseball Team from Mars.*

Walking along the row of books, I hear the floor creak. Its sound echoes off the low ceiling, like someone saying words aloud. I stop. The hot breeze rattles the frame of the window, making a humming sound. The screen vibrates back like an answering whisper.

Next in line are the chapter books. Because they are bigger and have their titles on the book spine, I can read the titles without pulling them from the shelves. My mother has a small bookshelf in her sewing room with three shelves of books. Grown up's books. I took some down to look at because the titles sounded like they'd be picture books. *The Long Goodbye. The Little Sister. The Big Sleep.* But there we no pictures. And they weren't for kids.

I read each case of chapter books like it is a page of a story, left to right, top to bottom. I pull out *Tales from Shakespeare.* Its spine makes a cracking sound as I open it. The illustrations look really old. Most of the stories are people's names. I keep this one in my hand as I move down the row. *Twenty Thousand Leagues Under the Sea.* The cover has some kind of submarine. Now I carry two books.

A fly buzzes around my head. A bead of sweat rolls into my eye and I feel the salt sting. My feet are hot and my sneakers feel tight. It's too hot to stay and I want to be outside. The fly is buzzing against the window, bouncing off of it, trying to get out. I go down the staircase and check out my books.

After I close the screen door behind me, I pause on the porch, feel the wind against my face, neck, arms. I sit on the glider, set my books next to me. It's a hot breeze, but it feels cool after being upstairs. I stand up and walk to my bike, get my rod and reel, my tackle box. I carry them in my left hand and hold the two books in my right hand.

Behind the library, past the cinder parking lot, is a wide concrete bridge, almost as long as a school bus, made from pouring concrete over a huge metal culvert. Miller Creek runs through it. Because the yard is flat, the creek is below me, down about ten feet of broken shale from where I stand looking. It takes two trips to get the books and fishing tackle down to the creek.

It's cool in the blue shade under the bridge. Going inside of the culvert is like going into a cave. Along the one side is a bank of concrete where I sit down. The scent of muck is strong. Miller Creek slows and widens here in a pool about two feet deep. Minnows dart and scatter. On the other side of the pool, I see a few mud chimneys the crayfish have built. But what I'm looking for in the water are bluegill, or if I'm lucky, a catfish. Either one, as long as I gut it, de-head it, and de-bone it, my mother will roll in corn meal and pan fry in butter.

I release the reel on my fishing rod and when the line goes slack, I remove the hook from the eyelet at the tip of the rod and free the line, like my dad taught me. The red and white wooden bobber gets removed because I don't want to fish close to the surface for bluegill. I open my tackle box and use the pliers my dad gave me to squeeze an extra lead sinker onto the line so the hook will lie on the bottom where the catfish feed. I take out a plastic bread bag, reach in, and remove a piece of white bread. Breaking off a piece the size of a movie ticket, I roll it into a tight ball the size of a cat's-eye marble that I work on to the hook. Now I'm ready to fish.

Hold the rigged fishing rod in my right hand, I let the line run slack a bit. I cast my bait, watch it sink, loop the slack around my index finger. If a catfish strikes, I'll watch the bobber and feel a quick tug.

I like fishing, but what I really come here for is to get books from the library. To find new books or read others by authors I like. People who see me with my fishing rod across the bars of my bike, and a bike basket filled with books, must think I'm fishing for books. And I sort of am. I have a better chance of finding a book I want to read than I do of catching a fish in this small creek.

I look at the books I've brought down from the library. Read the titles to myself. I settle on *Twenty Thousand Leagues Under the Sea*. I pick it up. The cloth cover of the book opens and I begin to read.

# A Cartographer's Tale

*You never know where a sentence will take you.*
                                    –Mary Oliver

The older I became, the quicker I could disappear down the street. And why not? A curious boy, I tended to wander off after a cat or a bird. If I was allowed to leave the yard, my parents insisted I stay on the sidewalk. When I was still too young to go to school, they told me to stay close to our house on West 191st Street, just off Puritas Drive. So there I would be, safe while riding my small bike, bored with the same five houses in one direction, six houses to the corner in the other, a limited back-and-forth route on my block which, from my mother's perspective, I was watchable. But as soon as my mother's back was turned, attention given to one of my brothers, changing a load of laundry, or talking on the phone, the world beyond my boundary called to me.

I would go farther than the two houses down to my Aunt Fran's house where I'd play with my cousin Danny who was a year younger than me. Near the end of the street, there was one vacant lot that had large maple trees and lots of bushes, places to look for blue jay feathers and robin's nests, or wildflowers such as spring violets or the tiger lilies of summer. If I got as far as the end of the street, I'd come to the Valley, as we called it, to the Cleveland Metroparks. The passable gap between two shrubs was a leafed turnstile, the beginning of a path where the older kids would go. It was like a doorway away from my known neighborhood into a wild and exotic landscape. I couldn't resist it.

I loved the twists and turns the paths took down into the valley, into the Rocky River Reservation, across the river from Little Metropolitan Golf Course, where the bridle path follows the valley to the horse stables. Brown rabbits abounded. Robins, cardinals, woodpeckers, sparrows and finches were abundant. Turtles, toads and frogs were common. Minnows and gar swam the shallows. Just about any third rock from the riverbank turned over in the shallows of the river exposed salamanders or newts. The Valley was my kindergarten, a living field guide I experienced before I went to school at St. Patrick's elementary school, scary with its small graveyard of aged and blackened stones, on the corner of Puritas Avenue and Rocky River Drive, the place from which I watched busses carrying people away from the known neighborhood to local stores, downtown, and beyond.

After moving west from the city, out to Avon Lake in Lorain County, I lived on a street that began near Lake Erie and ended in a forest of pin oak, silver maple, American elm, sassafras, white dogwood, and sumac. I spent whole days letting a path take me where it led.

Once I spent a morning following a garter snake. I roamed open fields and woods grown lush from the lake effect ecology, exploring the abandoned orchards of pear and apple trees, of grape vines and wild blackberry thickets. Before long I discovered how pin oak branches grew in a way that they were like a spiral staircase I could not only climb, but walk up to the highest branches. Sitting up there, looking down at birds was the closest I'd ever come to flying. Once I discovered old buckled sidewalks, poured by the WPA during the Depression in anticipation of suburban sprawl; finding monoliths or standing stones in Ireland or Scotland must leave one as speechless. The numerous ponds, just off some of my paths, were miraculous: teaming with tadpoles which metamorphosed into frogs, stone-like shells of secret turtles, and always the dodge and weave of the dragonflies and damselflies. The variety of Eastern songbirds living in the fields—oriole, finch, wren, blue birds, sparrows, thrushes, chickadees—were heard throughout my walks in the woods and fields.

These wanderings and experiences from my childhood have become a template for how I write. Helpful prepositions show me location, relationship, and connections—*at, by, with, near, over, under, around, across*—so that neither writer nor reader gets lost, while trees, bushes, and flowers along the path are adjectives defining depth, shadow, subtlety, hue. Simple sentences are sidewalks leading straight to surprising places. Expressed in the American vernacular, they sound as crisp, clean, or confident as if spoken by Harry Truman, or like clipped lines lifted from a William Carlos Williams poem. Such literary structures move me word by word from where I first begin a piece of writing to an ending that snaps an essay or story shut. Compound, complex, and compound-complex sentences are like roaming down a path in the woods. Once I start into such a complicated structure, there is often no telling where it will lead, what discoveries await: each turn on the path or phrase leads to a new dimension, each clearing or clause along the trail reveals another idea, some condition or tangent which invites the explorer in me to follow. Sentence fragments are stops and starts, the halting along the way to view something unexpected: a bird's egg fallen from a nest, the skull of a skunk, or the strange fungus named dead man's fingers that seems to reach up as if to grab ankles. The clean lines of independent clauses feel like deer trails crossing a path, offering alternatives I would not have imagined. Hard workers that I can depend upon without worry, they are as reliable as friends one has had since grade school. Just as paths lead to places, to cities, countries, and the world, so too do sentences lead to paragraphs, pages, and ultimately to books.

Henry David Thoreau trod paths of wonder at Walden. Charles Dickens walked familiar labyrinths in London's back streets. The wandering German writer W. G. Sebald nightly strode urban streets, country lanes, as well as memories and emotional fantasies. From roadways he'd walked in Dublin, Trieste, and Paris, James Joyce wove his textured tales. Virginia Woolf knew, from her microcosmic Bloomsbury blocks, all the doorways leading in and out of the varied lives lived there. William Faulkner layered infinite time upon time as his Mississippi country roads yielded the complexity of human relations. Emily Dickinson walked her small garden of a yard as if it were the world itself, as for her, it was. Walt Whitman bodied forth out from Long Island at fourteen, never stopping as he reached out with wide arms to bring all of North America into his poems. And Raymond Carver, in his late sober years, walked train tracks or the summer fields of the state of Washington, narrating the lyric moments of the wonder of his still being alive.

Writing takes me simultaneously on two profound paths, both into myself and out into the world. I become travel-wise and enriched in the same way that straying from the yard, off the sidewalk, used to give me the gift of adventure, exploration, and the ability to remain astonished. Because any pencil can be transformed into a walking stick, the act of writing is a journey, a process of discovery that evolves into the product or trace of the experience. Or as a kind of map to show me both the places I have been, as well as the places I have yet to go.

# Tasting a New Moon

*A croissant is dignified, born of tender care and craftsmanship. Bakers carefully layer the dough, paint on perfect proportions of butter, and then roll and fold this trembling croissant embryo with the precision of a Japanese origami master.*
–Association of French Bakers,
in response to Kanye West's criticism
of croissants in one of his songs

My mother grew up on Cleveland's near west side, eating home-baked loaves of white bread made from bleached flour. A child of the depression, she was captivated by the post war availability of timesaving, store-bought packages of sliced bread. As much as my two brothers and I couldn't get enough of our Grandma Ethel's fresh bread hand-sliced while still oven warm, we were keen to the ease of grabbing slices of Wonder Bread from the bread box, slathering them with Skippy or Jif peanut butter and Welch's Concord grape jelly. Often we'd have wax paper-wrapped sandwiches in our pockets or in paper bags when running out the door for a game of pick up baseball or to explore the woods and fields at the end of our street in Northeast Ohio.

Raising three boys, caring for her older sister Ruth, and maintaining a house while my father, who worked for Republic Steel as an industrial bolt salesman traveled eastern Ohio and western Pennsylvania, it was inevitable that ease would become my mother's culinary motto. When she had time, the cream puffs she made from scratch, using her mother's recipe, tasted exquisite. While she could make about two dozen different types of Christmas cookies, many of them passed-down family recipes, over the years she supplemented or replaced the Christmas tradition of making her own cookies from scratch. Instead, she drove her little blue Ford Falcon to the nearby Sparkle Supermarket to buy knock-out gingerbread men and assembly-line iced cut-outs.

So it was that my mother's idea of pastry baking eventually came to mean opening a package of prepackaged bake-at-home dough. Not only was it quick and easy, but it had the added joy of the scent of just-from-the-oven pastry which wafted from the small kitchen oven throughout the rest of our suburban ranch house. Her motherly duties seemed to her complete as she set a cloth towel-lined bowl of finished "fresh" bakery on the dinner table. It was at such a dinner that I encountered my first croissant.

But it wasn't an *actual* croissant. My mother had just popped open a thin cylinder constructed of cardboard with tin end caps that held packaged biscuit dough. After extruding the separated circular disks, she arranged the dough discs in rows on a cookie tray, rolled and reshaped them into something resembling a bell curve, then stretched the ends into points, sort of like gooey white smiles. She called them crescent rolls.

What I knew of crescents I'd discovered in *The Encyclopedia Britannica* that my parents purchased for my two brothers and me. In the volume that included the letter *E* for Egypt, I first read about the Fertile Crescent which included the Euphrates, Tigris, and the Nile rivers—synonymous with the Cradle of Civilization comprised of Upper and Lower Egypt, Mesopotamia, Assyria, Phoenicia, and Palestine. On the map, it resembled a quarter moon, either waxing or waning. On the table where we ate supper, the towel-lined bowl frequently held warm crescent dinner rolls.

But not just *any* dinner rolls. These were crescent rolls produced by the Pillsbury Company, which had come to national prominence in 1949 when it began hosting the National Bake-off at the Waldorf Astoria Hotel in New York City. A year later, they followed with the introduction, in the new supermarkets of the 1950s, of packaged dough offered in the "Give it a pop!" cylinders.

In what today would look like an episode of *Mad Men*, Rudy Perz, copywriter for Pillsbury's ad agency, imagined the wad of dough morphing into a small, pudgy, cartoon-like doll that came to life. Pillsbury had found its mascot, the Dough Boy, who was soon accompanied by a catchy sing-along jingle that celebrated, in an edited slant rhyme, how mothers could take "lovin'" from the "oven," and serve their families ready-made emotions every bit as warm as grandma's home-baked bread.

When my parents went out with their friends for dinner and drinks, my mother would leave my brothers and me with a special treat: Crescent Dogs, with the dough wrapped around an Oscar Meyer wiener and a folded slice of Kraft American cheese, always best served with a side of Tater Tots. Such culinary artistry was a clear indication that regional cuisine was changing in the Midwest during the early 1960s. Why waste time on local apple cider, fresh cake donuts, or clam bakes in the autumn when all you needed to do was whistle for the crescent dogs to come running?

As the use of refrigerated pastry grew, so too did its shelf life, from mere weeks to multiple months. Concurrent with such product development was the rise of margarine products—vegetable oils joined by beta carotene for yellow color and isolated natural butter compounds for a "real" imitation butter flavor—that, when added to refrigerated pastry, did not go rancid. Along this trajectory, Pillsbury went beyond the successful crescent roll, adding the new "butter flake" line that made the crescent roll more like its French cousin, that is, an *actual* croissant. But I was young then, eating those Crescent Dogs, and I did not know that what I took as real was merely a simulacrum, a false version of the actual.

Though my early childhood was along the Rocky River in Cleveland's "Emerald Necklace" Metroparks—a natural world of newts and under-rock salamanders, birds' nests and long-as-my-legs gar swimming leisurely against the slow current of the river —my parents moved after I finished first grade to Cleveland's western suburbs near Avon Point along the north coast of Lake Erie, once famous for Beach Park, easily accessible on the Lake Shore Electric Railway that ran to Lorain, Sandusky, and beyond along the north coast.

This was the great lake upon which my great grandfather James Higgins earned his living as a pleasure boat ship's captain, leaving from Cleveland's East Ninth Street Pier and going west to Detroit and east to Buffalo. My own childhood hours spent fishing from the concrete piers behind the coal burning electric power plant seemed a miniscule substitute for my great grandfather's Great Lakes life.

For some impulse impossible to articulate beyond my late adolescent understanding, and because of a cumulative grade point average that reflected my school years as an unmotivated student, I attended at the College in Steubenville for my freshman year. Steubenville was the first actual city in which I lived. In retrospect, I now see that I sought something more real than the semi-rural expanding suburb I had known until that time. The sequestered hilltop location of the college campus gave me a wide view of the old industrial city built along the slow-moving Ohio River, one far larger than the knee-deep-in-places Rocky River of my early childhood. This grand river was different, for it seemed to offer some vague truths awaiting my discovery.

For my sophomore year I transferred down river to attend Xavier University, a Jesuit institution in Cincinnati, the oldest large city in Ohio. From up in Eden Park, I could see the great swath of river below me. One curious day, I discovered an old leaning set of concrete steps I could walk down all the way to the near-downtown banks of the Ohio River. I marveled at the heady feeling of experiencing something so large and powerful as what I'd only seen in a book or an encyclopedia. In that moment I'd encountered an actual river. Looking up-river, I could see the future coming toward my nineteen-year-old self, see it momentarily flow slowly in front of me, and watch it, like my past, as it curved with the landscape and receded.

I spent a lot of time off campus that year. I was either down in Clifton, a bohemian district near the University of Cincinnati, or up in Mount Adams, an old German neighborhood that was experiencing early gentrification from capitalistic hippies and college stoners. Despite some gaps in my memory—this was the late 1960s, remember—I discovered a coffee shop that made espresso in small aluminum Bialetti makers, a method startlingly different from the instant coffee my parents, and I, constantly drank. Rich and strong as the imported chocolate I was discovering, complex and lush as the French wines I was trying, espresso was as compact and dense as the hashish my peers were smoking. My very impressionable nineteen-year-old taste buds were so dazzled that I spent star-struck hours peering into the demitasse of espresso as if into the eyes of a new lover. Once, though, my infatuation was interrupted when a barista asked me if I wanted anything to eat along with my espresso. Let me get you a croissant, she said.

It was love at first sight. The creamy almost-new snow color. The lightly browned tips and the top layer baked to crisp perfection. I pulled lightly from each horned end as if it was a pastry party favor and the croissant practically unraveled into two pieces in my hands, the lacy white interior delicate as a tatted doily, that decorative *frivolity* set on the china plate upon which sweet pastries are placed and presented. O, the breathtaking near weightlessness. O, the scent of—wait—*real* butter. And the taste was love at first bite: the sweet dough and buttered air of a croissant kiss.

This was the cotton candy of the pastry world. This the crescent waxing toward the full moon dream cuisine of the gourmand, bon vivant, epicurean, and hedonist. There, right there at my small table next to my notebook, sat an espresso and a croissant. But it was more than mere love: it was complete abandonment to my newfound bliss. From then on, I would always get a table for three. Bon appétit!

According to Prosper Montagné, author of the 1938 *Larousse Gastromonique: The Encyclopedia of Food, Wine & Cookery* (American translation, 1961, third printing), one finds, among the roughly 8,500 recipes scattered over its 1,100 pages, the alphabetical index for croissants on pages 322-323. Because the co-editor to the 1938 first edition, Philéas Gilbert, calls the volume "a reliable counsellor ready to be consulted," I accept the origin story of the croissant as presented by Montagné to be true. He dates it to the 1686 siege of Budapest by the Turks. Bakers busy at night making breads discerned the sound of their tunneling enemies and gave alarm, saving the city. To honor their heroic act, the bakers were rewarded with permission to create a special pastry that resembled the crescent moon emblem from the Ottoman flag. Oddly, Montagné does not narrate how this Hungarian delight traveled to become the distinct pastry of the boulangeries-pâtisseries of France. I'll assume word of mouth.

When I visited Paris in 2008, I was keen to taste as many true French croissants as possible, both early in the morning at the Montparnasse brasseries accompanied by espresso or in the well-lighted late-night brasseries joined by Medoc and Bordeaux wines. I proclaimed each croissant a tie with those previously sampled and ordered more. Paris, in my mind, was home to the absolute and ultimate croissant experience, comparable to a trip to Mecca or Wrigley Field. But then in 2014, my wife Molly and I went to Old Québec City, Canada, described in my *Lonely Planet* guidebook as the next best thing to a European walled city, and very French at that.

The Chateau des Tourelles is an 1898 turreted four-story house converted into a bed and breakfast. It is conveniently located a leisurely fifteen-minute walk down Rue Saint-Jean toward the Porte Saint-Jean entrance in the castle-like walls of Old Québec. The turret of the Chateau itself leads circularly up five stories and a narrow hallway to the flat roof where guests find a wooden deck with iron railings. The deck offers a panoramic view of Église Saint-Jean-Baptiste, the city streets, the huge St. Lawrence River, and the low, blue Laurentian mountains that lie north of the city. Our second night on the roof, my wife Molly and I finished a bottle of lush Two Sisters Niagara River Cabernet Franc and opened a Cuvée from Ste Pétronille Vineyards on Ile D'Orléans. The next morning, we decided to have lunch on the rooftop, so we set out to purchase some local goat cheese plus a baguette or croissant to have with the rest of the Cuvée.

We asked for shopping recommendations. William, the young French-Canadian manager of the Chateau, told us that almost every block in the Old City had a cheese shop, but there was really only one place to buy croissants: Le Pain Grüel, an artisanal bakery on Rue Saint-Jean known for its organic ancient grain breads. When we asked him for the address, William laughed and told us to follow our noses.

Walking down the sidewalk inside Québec's Old City walls, I wondered whether Le Pain Grüel bakery actually existed, or if it was some sort of French Canadian boulangerie mirage.

Then, at the same moment, Molly and I stopped on the sidewalk.

We stood absolutely still.

We raised our heads, sniffing the air like scent hounds ready for a chase.

An intense fresh-baked bread scent intoxicated us, drew us enchantedly toward the inset spring-green door as we walked, like string-operated marionettes, into Le Pain Grüel bakery.

Warm oak cabinets, earth-colored tile floors and counters, and rich red trim: it felt perfect for this *boulangerie*. We sampled small bites of day-old rye bread, stood transfixed as soldiers at attention in front of baskets of baguettes standing like swords raised in defense against the mediocrity of commercial bakery.

Then I turned and saw the cooling rack, a treasure chest laden with spilled golden crescent coins.

I stared like a man entranced. I wasn't breathing. I actually couldn't talk. Instead, I could only point, and did.

How many croissants, the baker asked.

Two, I croaked.

No, three, I said.

Make it four, Molly added.

After picking up a round of local goat brie and crisp green apples from a small grocery on Rue Saint-Jean, we walked back up to the Chateau des Tourelles, our strides as long as baguettes, our hearts rising like new loaves, our hands entwined like braided bread dough.

Though the sun on the rooftop deck was warm, a cool late May breeze touched our necks. I looked up from the St. Lawrence River, as magical and mesmerizing as the grand Ohio River had seemed when I was younger. I turned my focus to the sky, seeking a leftover sliver of moon, but there was none. Molly and I chewed half slices of apple, each of us lulling in a gluten buzz.

My crescent roll journey was ending, my archetypal narrative was coming to its final point of arrival, like an errant knight's quest completed. The buttery piece of light dough I'd removed from the center of the croissant with my left hand was soft and pliant like just-steamed mussels nesting in a warm ceramic bowl, or like the soft wax tears from poppies used to make opium. I was hooked.

# Two

*Even in Kyoto, hearing the cuckoo's cry, I long for Kyoto.*
–Matsuo Bashō

# Ohio Ode

An intersection of states and lakes and rivers. Of place and promontory and plains and potential. Of history recalled and history in-the-making. Of conservatives and progressives, independents and non-voters. Ohio is such a collection of cultures, contrasts, contradictions, juxtapositions, environments, ecologies, politics, and social status that it reads like its own encyclopedia.

The state's north coast is concurrently the country's north coast on the water border with Ontario; the eastern boundary is the Ohio River which was once the boundary of the expanding US wilderness; southern and southeastern Ohio is distinctly Appalachian—mountainous, rugged, and often ecologically exploited; western Ohio is where the Great Plains begin their reach toward the Rockies.

Ohio's name comes from what the Iroquois people who historically inhabited the region called the "Great River." This large, grand, great waterway has since come to be called the Ohio River. The name is both a literal description of what one sees when looking at the Ohio River for the first time, as well as a redundancy, for etymologically it means the Great River river. Since the name of the river has been applied by European explorers and settlers to mean the land it borders, it is metaphorical in that one thing (the "Great River" by name) is in fact actually the land and terrain itself. Rhetorically, such a description is a synecdoche, for it speaks of a part of something (a section of the "Great River") to mean the whole thing (the entire "Great River"), yet is concurrently metonymical, for it associates the general term "Ohio" (meaning the "Great River") with the thing it stands for, that is, the physical territory of the state of Ohio.

The rhetoric confuses the metaphorical and poetic nature of the name's origin and its acquired meaning. On a language level, Ohio denotes the state itself, yet it carries the connotation of the river as subtext or ghost or echo: but that is poetry, the simultaneous multiplicity of meaning. The name "Ohio" is a word which when spoken aloud has a sound that echoes the word itself, as in the way that the name Ohio (a state) seems to echo the original sound of river water rushing or rippling (the "Great Water"). Moreover, Ohio is analogously shaped sort of like a poem on a page, with clearly established functions for what's at the top and bottom of a poem (the opening and closure), while the left and right define margin and line break.

The shape of the state is also that of a shield, both a sheltering herald and a visual example of its recognized and understood separate parts. As a result, Ohio is stable, solid, and steadfast, which contributes to its cautious and relatively predictable Midwestern character located between what was once, to its east, the English colonies that revolted to become the original United States and, to its west, the expanding frontier as territories became states, as Ohio did in 1803. Yet the shield-like shape of Ohio also looks like an inverted keystone or capstone, the stone wedge at the top of a masonry arch, the key that locks the weighty structure solid. As such, the keystone is the crux, or heart, of the arch, or as a metaphor for Ohio, it is central to the structural system. Granted, Pennsylvania, the state that shares the Ohio River as a border, was called the Keystone State after its geographical location among the freed American Colonies along the Atlantic. Ohio's inverse shield-like keystone, however, locks tight the nation's north coast, connecting the original colonies, the Great Lakes, and the Great Plains.

The divisions in Ohio are less east-west, however, and clearly more north-south, a common pattern on the crest and heralds on shields. Because the Ohio River-Mississippi River was an aquatic version of modern highways, travelers settled Southeast Ohio's Appalachian Plateau along the (then) Virginia border, as well as Ohio's southern border with Kentucky, with Ironton near the weighty lowest point. To the southeast, Cincinnati grew in the early 1800s as steamboats made both the economy and the population boom, leading to its nickname as the Queen City, and Cincinnati's self-identification as the Gateway to the South, evident in its slow-paced sultry summers. Cleveland is Ohio's great northern economic and cultural powerhouse, which grew as a port city when the Great Lakes moved goods and people from Chicago all the way to the Atlantic by way of the Saint Lawrence River. To balance the economic and cultural clout of Cincinnati and Cleveland, Columbus (another letter "C") was established as the compromise capital of Ohio in 1816, a common ground for resolving the power struggle. Like the Midwest itself, such a compromise was a cautious and predictable recognition of the natural split of the state.

While the sporting world knows Columbus for professional soccer, as well as collegiate football and basketball of The

Ohio State University, both Cincinnati and Cleveland have professional football and baseball teams that regularly compete, leading to the Ohio Cup rivalry, awarded to the winner of annual interleague play between the two major league Ohio baseball teams. It seems somehow fitting that a cursory glance at a map of Ohio shows what looks like the home plate found on any baseball field in the world. And in a state that accepts its separated sense of identity, good sporting activity is a heathy recognition, somewhat like the annual softball game held in Washington, D.C. between the Democrats and the Republicans.

Baseball is an American game, as the poet Walt Whitman stated following the end of the Civil War, or the War between the States. "It is our game," he stated, one "connected with our national character," for it can "repair our losses" as needed. While Whitman spoke of the immediacy of baseball, poet Donald Hall praised its historical and generational value, stating that "Baseball is continuous, an endless game of repeated summers, joining the long generations of all the fathers and all the sons."

Ohioans in their turn step into the batter's box of life, tap the head of the bat on home plate, than lift it up, awaiting fate's pitch: the luck of walking to first base, the sharp ache of a wild pitch, a ground ball out, a breaking ball that leads to a strike, a swing and miss, or better, a hit that gets the batter on base, or best yet, a seemingly impossible and inexpressibly fantastic home run. Regardless of the outcome, it is the playing that matters, being the batter stepping into the box and taking a swing, even if only for the experience of doing so.

Ohio writer James Thurber once advised, "look neither back to the past with anger, nor towards the future with fear, but look around with awareness." Ohioans can look around and choose to walk in any direction, and in doing so, will encounter varied landscapes, unexpected intersections and juxtapositions, and complex regional identities. The result will be an awareness, a realization, an epiphany. Or possibly a greater appreciation of how to look, without apprehension, yet with open mindedness, toward the future.

# Out of Alsace

Always the hunger came to Monsieur Messmer. Nightly, it visited his sleep, where he dreamed of arriving in new lands, places where orchard rows filled with fruit and bees. Mornings he stood, vaguely mesmerized, regarding the transformation of an empty sky into a cumulus cloud as he sang his soon-to-be immigrant song.

The taste for movement called to Madame, his wife, among lines of cabbage and tarragon, along rows of d'Anjou pears, regaling her with its spun-golden stories. She canned the future in tin-lidded jars to survive on when hope would become the new troubadour. Hunger's sweet mouth slipped seeds into her earbud, pasting leaves on fingertips and tongues, spoke daily to the empty pod of her body.

Monsieur Messmer was one of the one-in-ten in Alsace who was French. The German occupiers gave them leave to leave. His native Strasbourg rode the border like a saddle, a horse balanced athwart a tightrope. He held the reins loosely, ready, reading the situation. Did Paris await his return? Would their fellow citizens open their arms like crucifixes or scarecrows? Can cities be caught as easily as fish or trains?

The national narrative told tales of ex-patriots, but not episodes of those who emigrated. Men who go briefly will always be prodigal sons welcomed into open arms upon returning, but men who leave for life look back to see arms

folded over chests, hard faces and fists. Monsieur unsaddled
the piebald mare and changed nations like he would change
trains.

With brothers and babies, baggage and bottles of vin
blanc, the Messmers and their child Emile left Ste. Marie
aux Mines, accompanied by Monsieur's brothers, Louis
and Alois. Together they took the train across Spain and
caught the British ferry from Gibraltar, arriving in Algiers,
the mouth of Algeria, seeking the French enclave's sweet
tongue and enfolding arms of common welcome. What
did they miss? The smell of the farm fields wet with spring
rains? Vineyards and dairies, orchards and wineries? Onion
quiche, snails in sauerkraut, pate de foie gras, civet of hare
with noodles?

But the heat there was a buttoned Navy wool coat. But the
poppies withered in the bright garden. Monsieur Messmer
stood disruptively mesmerized, his eyes scanning a terrain
of hourglass sand that made an ocean that surrounded them,
isolated as a French island in a sea of sand.

For seven years the brothers entered the earth's cool belly,
miners loading bauxite into carts on tracks they pushed
toward the bitter mouth of the mine, delivered by men pale
as potatoes. Like a lightning flash, the sky blinded them.
The brothers were given the common earnings and sailed
toward the new land to look for new jobs, better pay, more
opportunities in America. Monsieur Messmer toiled and
saved, while Madam birthed two more children in the Arab
Maghreb.

How hard to sing of relocation when a parched throat
arrives. It is debauched to a citizen in exile, a mime of a
miner or stranger in the street, an ex-patriot at the turnstile,

seven years of waiting, of wishing, of wanting. Always the hunger whispered in their ears.

The Messmers settled into steerage, the belly of the boat dark and close as a mineshaft. The Atlantic cradled the steamer in its crossing, swelling by whitecap by Azores by gull by birthing-woman by breech by stillborn. The ocean was handed the swaddled baby. Madame was heart cut and heart wet in the ocean spray, heart dry in the night when the prow with its steerage where they rode rose like a swing then fell like a sledge, the clash of steel and wave reverberating in them. They were all of one belly, all of one loss. The baby's name was lost at sea.

Monsieur Messmer arrived visibly mesmerized at the mouth of the Cuyahoga River. The family disembarked on a riverbank of gritty industry cluttered with the sad shanty dwellings of Irishtown Bend near where Moses Cleveland's ferry first crossed the crooked river that cleaved the land. But the reunited family esprit took them south to farmlands above the river valley, arriving in Berea.

Lush fields of daisies and sassafras, maple and ash greeted them. Then orchards and vineyards. Gardens and coops. Cellar and barn and springhouse. Farmhouse. The dandelion taste of poverty left as spring came bearing gifts on warm summer storm clouds: spinach and radish, rhubarb and asparagus, trellised snap peas and rouge d'Hiver romaine lettuce. Together the Messmers felt the dream lean against their foreheads like soft rain, the residual image of arrival wiping their faces.

The next baby came to Madame in a dream of seed as her liminal waist became an opening door. Monsieur and Madame turned into Mr. and Mrs. as her open face experienced the transformation of an empty cask into a filled barrel as she sang of Caroline, a first-born-in-new-land child.

The old uncles, Alois and Louis Messmer, sat in the kitchen in Caroline Messmer Higgins' house on Cleveland's near west side, playing cards and cursing in their native French. They laid down the aces and eights like sidewalk slates. Vin Blanc poured into juice glasses from which they economically sipped. The cigarettes came to them from their English-speaking grandniece Genevieve, who rolled them for a penny each. They cut the face cards for luck.

Their grandniece, who was my mother, put the pennies in a small crystal vase that she set on the windowsill where the sunlight came to it like a worldly lover telling her stories of her bright future.

Rooted in Ohio, I am ensnared in its present moment. History, if I summon you with incantations, paper the walls with my family tree, will you liberate me, feed me? These Messmers who hypnotize my lost past are strange to me, gray faces in fading photographs of old-world ancestors lost among the displaced and disappearing members of the grand narrative of my family on my mother's mother's side.

How I miss you now, my Alsatian ancestors I never knew. Strasbourg, Nancy, Mülhausen. You who maintained ponds and developed pisciculture in Kolmar. Stuffed pike, frogs' leg soup, crayfish flan, blue trout au vin. I would dine with you if I could, listen to your immigration stories over *pâté and plums, kugelhopf and kirsch.*

Meeting you here on the page where I write, you family of Alsatian strangers, I raise glasses of sweet muscat and framboise, toast you with gewürztraminer, pinot gris, and reisling as the sunlight from the window illuminates the glasses, transforming them into incandescent lights that shine upon the past, offering a prologue into the future.

# Desperados

In the mid-1970s my girlfriend and I were living cheap in Denver. We rented a bottom floor apartment of an old house off of East Colfax back before Denver's old Capitol Hill neighborhood became gentrified. We were young then, two kids from the far western suburbs of Cleveland, and everything seemed as possible as the romantic plots of afternoon matinees at the movie theater.

I was working for a run-out-of-the-garage landscaping company, saving money to go to school part time winter quarter so I could finish my teaching degree program. My girlfriend worked as a legal secretary for a top-floor law firm. Between the two of us, we made enough to cover the bills and hit the bars. Enough to go to some concerts at Red Rocks on summer nights to see Tom Waits or Jackson Browne or the Eagles. At the end of the month we still had some money left. We joked that we were living like characters out of the movies.

One hot Friday afternoon in late summer, I was in line at the drive-thru bank waiting to cash my paycheck. Half a dozen vehicles idled in front of me and in my rear-view mirror I could see a few more cars behind me. We were like a parade anxious to start the weekend.

I was driving a used '68 Dodge short bed pickup truck, a red one with a three-speed manual transmission. It was great for going off-road in the Rockies. The truck had lots of working miles on it, sure, but the engine hadn't lost its throaty growl. The shady landscaping company I was working for offered to lease it back for a couple hundred bucks a month. I signed on because I was twenty-four and it was the best deal I had going. I got paid enough to cover the bank loan and the gas tank was always full. I couldn't beat that deal with a shovel.

I rolled down the passenger side window and let the late afternoon air in. The strong Colorado sun centered in the huge stark blue Western sky felt good on my left arm, on my face. I turned up the dashboard radio because it was the Eagles, my soundtrack band at the time. I sang along with the line, *He was just a hired hand, workin' on the dreams he planned to try.*

The envelope sent by pneumatic tube from the teller inside the bank arrived. I opened it and put the receipt for the money I'd deposited, plus some cash, in my wallet. My next stop was a downtown bar three blocks down and two blocks over where I'd meet my girlfriend for Friday-after-work drinks.

After I left the bank parking lot, I swung the pickup onto the flow of the one-way street. I crossed over two lanes to the left and pulled under the shade of a tree along the downtown block with free parking, rolled up the window, and cut the engine.

I stepped out of the truck and turned to use my ignition key to lock the driver's side door. It was cheaper than getting the lock fixed.

Something hard pressed against my lower back.

"Your money or your life," growled a man's gruff voice close to my left ear.

I couldn't see him, but the smell of his cigarette breath hung as heavy as the menace of his words. I pictured a moody Humphrey Bogart or a bad-ass Marlon Brando pushing a pistol against my spine. The image seemed somehow comical under these circumstances. Then I did what I do when I get nervous. I laughed.

"This ain't funny," he said.

Never rattle a robber, I knew that. But my mind started flashing with movie images of tough detectives and rough cowboys, men who I could see—men who suddenly looked like me—spinning in an instant, bringing hard elbows to surprised jaws, mouths, and throats. I saw myself, this guy's gun suddenly in my hand, pointing it back at him now, barking "Don't move!" But I knew that scenario was ludicrous.

What if it was not even a real gun, I wondered. Maybe it was a fake, a prop, and this robbery a trick. Maybe all he really had was a roll of pennies. But what if I was wrong and he had a real gun? And the moment he felt me try to spin around to fight back, he'd pull the trigger and shoot me in the back.

"You're right," I said, "this isn't funny."

"Yeah," he said.

I didn't say anything else. This was his show. He was the scriptwriter. And the director. He had the starring role. In this scene I was the B grade actor without a body double. I stayed quiet.

But he didn't say anything either. So there we stood, locked static in a moment, like boxers in a photograph.

I wondered why we'd gone off the robbery script. Had he only written it this far? Hadn't he watched this scene in a thousand movies? Was this his first hold up? Was he a robbery novice, an amateur crook, a crime virgin? Someone playing out a part he'd never rehearsed, making it up and improvising as he went along? What if he was as scared—or more scared—than I was?

The Colorado sun turned the truck's window into a mirror. My eyes glanced over quickly and I saw this short guy behind me. Saw his denim jacket. His Pittsburgh Pirates baseball cap. His Fu Manchu moustache. His silver mirrored aviator sunglasses in which, if I've had time to squint and focus, I might have seen my own reflection looking back at myself in the truck's window. In a half-second my eyes darted back, straight ahead, and there I was, looking at my not-very-self-assured self in the eyes, imagining looking at myself through the aviator-glassed eyes of this robber.

"I don't know what you look like, man," I said, "and I plan to keep it that way."

He was quiet. Maybe thinking about what I said. Or if I meant what I'd said.

"Good," he said.

Then he was silent again.

I needed to keep the action moving before it got weird. The last thing this scene needed was an undercurrent of anxiety and edgy tension.

"You want my billfold," I said, forcing myself to speak evenly.

"Yeah," he said.

"Ok," I said. "It's in my back-right pocket. Do you want to take it out," I asked, "or should I do it?"

"You," he said.

"Ok," I said.

"Move slow so I can see your hands," he said, "And no sudden moves."

I leaned my left hand against the truck for balance, then used my right hand to hold my billfold out and away from my body.

Stick to the script, I thought, don't ad lib.

But it was already too late.

I heard myself say, "Hey man, can you just take the cash? It's a pain in the ass to get a new driver's license, you know?"

The only sound was of cars driving passing us on the one-way street.

"Yeah," he said. "That'd suck."

Then he laughed, *heh, heh, heh*, like that. Like we were buddies on the set between takes, sharing jokes and cigarettes.

"Open the wallet slow and take out the cash," he said. He pressed what felt like a gun harder against my lower spine. My face reflected in the truck window was a close-up shot now. I could see lines of sweat running down from my temples.

"Ok," I said as I brought my right hand carefully up against the side of the truck.

I opened the wallet by working my fingers and spread the pouch so that he could see the cash, seven twenty-dollar bills. I felt the money leave the wallet, followed by the wallet leaving my hand.

"Thanks," he growled into my ear, "Asshole."

He said it in a way that wasn't a threat, but more like an afterthought, like a bad actor who dropped a line after missing his cue and had to say something because the camera was rolling.

I could feel myself being pushed. What began with a slow motion shot rapidly accelerated.

My forehead hit the truck cab.

It wasn't hard enough to break the skin, but man, it hurt like a son of a gun.

I looked up and saw my wallet fly over me like a clay pigeon, then fall and skid along the street. The baseball-capped, denim-clad figure was running from me, going the wrong way on a one-way street. He ran past the drive-thru bank, cut down an alley, and disappeared between a brick apartment building and a convenience store.

"Asshole," I said.

I meant him when I said it, but I also meant me too.

I went and picked up my wallet. Then I started walking to the bar to meet my girlfriend.

The Broker was located on 17ᵗʰ Street inside a steel-blue bank vault in the brick-walled basement of what had been a Denver cattle bank in the late eighteen-hundreds. I guess being in a sort of walk-in safe deposit box was supposed to make patrons feel safe, feel valued.

I stopped at the bottom of the wooden staircase when I first got there and went into the Men's before I went into the bar. I splashed cold water on my face, held a couple of soaked paper towels to my forehead.

In the restroom mirror I could see a small lump starting to rise on my forehead. In a day or two the red splotch would be a blue-black bruise. While I felt around inside my wallet, I knew it was not the fluorescent light that made me look pale.

After I left the restroom, I made a stop by the Juke box and dropped in some of the quarters I always carried in the watch pocket of my Levi's, then punched the buttons. There were some songs I needed to hear. I nodded my head to the lines, *Don't you draw the queen of diamonds boy, she'll beat you if she's able.*

By the time I was safely deposited on a bar stool, my hands were shaking pretty bad. In the old, silvered mirror on the oak plank wall behind the bartender I could see that I appeared calm, just another working man easing into a weekend.

But my stomach was flipping around like a car that'd gone off the road. Too much zany adrenalin racing around in my body trying to figure out what to do with itself, how to bust out, how to slow down. *Take it easy,* Glenn Frey sang, *don't let the sound of your own wheels drive you crazy.*

I knew what to do now. I pictured it clearly. I'd seen this a hundred times before in the movies.

"Give me two shots of Jack Daniels," I said.

"One of those for the girlfriend when she arrives?" asked the bartender, who knew me as a regular of Friday paydays.

"Nope. She can order what she wants when she gets here," I said.

The bartender set the Daniels twins in front of me.

I slammed the first one down. The way it felt going down my throat was a good burn that stole my breath.

My hands stopped shaking, so I took out my wallet, removed my credit card, and tossed it on the bar.

"Put her on my tab," I said.

In the old, beveled mirror in front of me I could see the reflection of the growing number of people coming in from work. Stockbrokers, lawyers, secretaries, real estate agents, managers, all being joined by friends, wives, lovers, everyone looking like they were living the good life. I guess that I was too, for I was relatively uninjured and quite alive after a robbery. Around me, the clanging glasses and servers' metal trays, the flames of lighters for table candles or cigarettes, the young and old faces lit by the blue light from TV screens created a panorama of extras among which I had been cast.

Along the bar, bottles of liquor gathered together like an ensemble of actors in a film version of a Charles Bukowski novel. Illuminated from spotlights above, the bourbon, vodka, amaretto, and gin were diamonds and gems in a jewelry store display case, bright colors sparkling and refracting. The glint and dazzle reminded me of theater marquees on opening night. The jukebox played *We may lose and we may win, we will never be here again.* It could have been the final soundtrack of a movie.

As I drank that second shot of Tennessee whiskey, I swear I saw the closing credits of a film scroll down the mirror's silver screen.

# The Valdemar Car

A hard rain is coming furiously down on the windshield. Even with the car wipers at top speed, I can barely see the taillights of the cars in front of me. I'm driving my Datsun B 210 on I-90 West, ready to exit at Clifton Boulevard in Cleveland. Regular rain on the roof sounds like hail, so this thunderstorm sounds like an avalanche of golf balls. I'm entombed in a deafening dark gray box.

Looking into the blinding shower for the exit sign, I see a large blue-black rectangle suddenly rise up from the road.

What the hell? It's a flying wet carpet of death; it wants to wrap me like a mummy.

When it lands on my windshield, the wipers stop, making a straining and dying whirring sound. I can't see a thing. My heart alternates between beating and stopping. *You murderous piece of steel*, I shout at the car, *are you trying to kill me?* The wipers hum in reply.

I turn the wheel to the right, to the berm, and put both feet on the brake as the car leaves the highway and slides onto the soggy grass. The engine stalls. I catch my breath. The sound the car makes is like sarcastic laughter.

In the mid-1970s Datsun marketed the B-210 "Sunny" in North America as a lightweight, sporty little hatchback with a 4-speed that got almost 50 mpg on the highway. I bought mine used as a drive-to-work car to get to school.

The car was as green as a plastic toy frog. Back near the gas cap was a small yellow "Honeybee" decal. Smiling and accompanied by ellipsis-like dashes, both bee, and car by association, were flying happily along.

Embarrassed by the bizarre mesmerizing color and cartoonish bee, I considered dinging the bee with another car, just enough to get my insurance to pay for a repair and repaint. If my deductible had been lower, I'd have done it.

Edgar Allen Poe's short story "The Facts in the Case of M. Valdemar" was published simultaneously in December 1845 in both *The American Review* and *The Broadway Journal*, which Poe himself edited. The narrator is a mesmerist known only as "P—" who uses magnetism to hypnotize Ernest Valdemar, a writer, at the very moment of his death from tuberculosis. P— suspends Valdemar in the hypnogogic state at the threshold of consciousness between waking and sleeping, a lucid dream state in which Valdemar is aware that he is dreaming, but not actually dead. For seven months Valdemar's body is cold, pale, bluish, still. Yet he speaks, P— says, as if from a vast distance.

"I am dying," Valdemar states, "Let me die!" But P—is ever the scientist, so the experiment continues. Valdemar keeps asking to die, until one day Valdemar claims that he is dead. In an attempt to speak with a dead man, P—breaks the spell and—this is a Poe story, remember—all seven months of existing in a suspended state instantaneously catch up with Valdemar. He liquefies and splashes to the floor.

Though the gruesome ending shocked Poe's readers, Elizabeth Barrett Browning wrote to Poe, praising his ability to make "horrible improbabilities seem familiar." Yet Poe had surprisingly published the piece not as a work of fiction, but as a scientific hoax, a sort of 19<sup>th</sup> Century predecessor of the Orson Welles 1938 radio broadcast of his adaptation of the H. G. Welles 1898 novel *The War of the Worlds*. Both men were berated for duping their respective audiences, yet residual anger over Poe's hoax remains to this day, refusing to die.

Two design flaws in the Datsun B-210 always tricked me. The first were the lousy shock absorbers that turned the car into a rocking-horse when I had to brake quickly. The other was the erratic ignition.

I'd put the key in and turn it, but nothing would happen. I'd take the key out, put it back in, and turn it again. Nothing.

Again I'd try, and the B-210 would respond. *Let me die,* it would say. *I am dead,* it would say.

Running late for work, as usual, I habitually set a ceramic cup of hot coffee on the roof while loading my briefcase and my bookbag into the back seat before driving away. As I accelerated up the street, I'd hear the cup sliding toward the back of the car, followed by the short second when the cup was suspended in air. Then I'd hear the crash, the splash, the mess.

The young Puerto Rican girl from Lorain and her brother return from test driving my Datsun with its taped-to-the-inside window piece of cardboard announcing Car For Sale, All Offers Considered. Her hands clutch below her throat, wide-eyed in wonder at the little honeybee of a car. Her brother shakes his head in disbelief at the totally shitty shocks.

They walk a few feet away, near the coffee stains on the street, to talk. Her hand points now and then to the car. He stands solid, feet spread, arms folded across his chest.

They walk back and the brother pulls hundred-dollar bills from his shirt pocket and sets them on the hood of the Datsun. The color of the money blurs into the green finish of the car so that I can only distinguish the difference by the small, rug-like shape of the bills.

The girl gets in the driver's side, clicks her seatbelt, and turns to her brother in the passenger seat with a big smile. When she puts the key in the ignition, it starts right up.

They drive smoothly down the street, the car buzzing along like a honeybee. This former hoax of a car that once begged to expire seems suddenly sprite and young and joyous.

No coffee cup crashes and dies on the street behind it. I feel duped.

# Death of the Fugitive Charles Floyd

East Liverpool, Ohio
October 22, 1934

Leaves fall along rows of tree trunks in the late October orchards. The last apples hang, red as the cheeks of girls and boys playing in the first snow of winter.

In town, stunted skeletons of burr oak, catalpa, and Osage orange irregularly line the waste lots located along the train tracks. Yellow jackets buzz, ready to swarm relentlessly if their underground nests are threatened.

The afternoon sun pushes the dark shapes of a brick apartment building and a clapboard car repair garage into square black cells across a rutted alley. Each is as quiet as a mausoleum, empty as a robbed bank vault.

Inside one of the rectangular shadows, a man in a wool suit, tie, and an overcoat stands still. His head is turned slightly. He listens intently for the sound of anyone approaching. He hears a blue jay squawk, hears a crow caw. He catches his breath.

The man darts from the small cloak of darkness and in an instant, he is again absorbed into the tentative safety of the next dark rectangle. He releases his breath. Listens. Checks for his .38 Colt automatic in his pocket. Listens again.

He knows if he can make it down this alley, past corn stalks standing like rusty bayonets, he'll get to the Ohio River. He knows he's a strong swimmer, the only other thing beyond the Colt he can trust. The Ohio River is wide, but he knows there are few currents there to catch him.

On the other side of the river are the ridges and hollows of West Virginia. He trusts in the compassion of poor folk who will take him in, hide him, lie for him. They always do.

They've heard how, back in Oklahoma, he burned mortgage notes in bank managers' trash cans before he ran to the getaway car with a bag of money in one hand, his pistol in the other.

The man hears a crow call, followed by a second one, then a third. Hears a chorus of blue jays grow louder as they fly closer. Hears an automobile backfire. He bolts from the safety of the shadow, exposed as if caught in the spotlight of a police car full of US Marshalls who are packed together shoulder to shoulder, the way bullets fit into loaded guns.

# Quiet

Inside the 1905 brick foursquare house in the Vassar Park neighborhood in Canton, the quiet calms me. A particular kind of near noiselessness can be found in old houses in the Midwest during wintertime. People outside are rarely heard unless it's the old woman who walks her three mutt dogs, talking to them all the while. Or teenagers walking up the alley, smoking and joking. A school bus in the afternoon offers a brief interlude. Inside, the furnace kicks on or off. The metallic tick of the ducts cooling down. Drops of rain or icy snow on the windowpane. The steaming prediction of a tea kettle's whistle. The floor creaking when the old dog stretches then jumps up onto the bed to nap. The light purr of the laptop.

Alternatively, a house can be mute. An extended pause between the winds and leaves of autumn. The hush of a house late at night when the doors are locked, lights off, the bored dog settled: a tranquil shush before sleep comes. Still as a university library where the only audible sound is of the periodic turning of pages of paper. Silent as a church in the dark before dawn, dimly lit by the flicker of votive candles, a noiseless space for repose or reprieve or meditation or confession or calm. Silence is both the context for prayer and prayer itself. Even if you don't believe in prayer, you can still believe in quiet.

"Grandma just turned a hundred and three this year," my neighbor tells me.

Her grandmother, a frail, aged woman with white hair, leans on her wooden cane. She squints at me and nods her head in affirmation.

I stand there nodding back. My neighbor's car's exhaust pipe makes a pinging sound as it cools down.

The midsummer day is Ohio humid, and I hear the highway in the distance, a lawn mower starting up on the next block. I can see a guy down the street cleaning his car in the driveway, hear the twang of the country song he's listening to while he works.

"It sure is a different world now than the one you grew up in, isn't it, Grandma?" my neighbor asks.

Her grandmother stares up at a commercial airliner chalking its line across the sky. Without looking back at us, she replies, "It used to be a lot quieter."

I only listen to the radio if I'm working outside in my yard. If so, it's a Cleveland Indians baseball game. It keeps me company and moves along inning by inning, measuring time in a way that is different from the hand of a watch or a digital display.

Radios never stop speaking. Dead air is unacceptable because filling up the space with sound is a measure of money. Silence is its nemesis. I don't enjoy the jabber of disc jockeys or talk show hosts or news or the insistence of commercials. It makes me nervous. It's manic. Worse still is having the radio on in the car, especially in heavy traffic, and at such times I am thankful that I can pop Bach into the CD player and round off the rough edges of the hectic and erratic traffic.

Yet I do like the contrapuntal warm fall days, driving down streets when the leaves have fallen and dried, my windows rolled down, listening to the song of the wheels on the road surface, the crush of leaves, the percussion from the scrape of sticks and twigs along the curb.

After a wave crashes and recedes, silence arrives split-secondly before the next crest approaches. Our world is louder and fuller and busier than the history of humans seems able to sustain. Sounds of cell phones and ads and entertainment and traffic and displacement and conflict and turmoil have become the soundtrack for our era. So much noise makes us uneasy, anxious, tense. The last safe, comforting, renewing space we have left is in moments of silence, wherever we can find them along the shore of a calm day on the Great Lakes. Or on a forest path. Or next to an Ohio farm pond. Or in a wood-paneled home library where I sit, paused, before I pick up a pen and begin writing.

# Into the Bargain

The northeast Ohio sleet streaks and blurs the Christmas lights at the mall. Shapes of cars and pickups and vans in the parking lots look like snow-covered wrapping-papered presents. I'm circumnavigating the suburban mall in overlapping loops, looking in the outlier locations where shoppers find low price specialties that fall outside the range of standard commercial fare.

This year it's could be called the Book Bazaar. Last year it might have been Pop Up Paperbacks. Another year, Holiday Book Market. The names change but the concept is the same: each is an impulse buyer's paradise for readers who look for good books at give-away prices.

Finding seasonal booksellers like Book Bazaar offers the joy of discovering new writers or old friends, all affordable on a schoolteacher's salary. These are the Christmas presents I buy for myself. Residual traces of hunting and gathering intersect as I walk the aisles and book tables, alert and open to possibility.

Sometimes I find an amazing deal, like *Helen Frankenthaler: A Paintings Retrospective*, published in a coffee table hardback by Abrams and the Modern Art Museum of Fort Worth, which sells retail for seventy-five dollars but is marked down to only seven ninety-nine. The Frankenthaler was a close-out with a remainder mark slashed across the bottom of the book with a black Sharpie. I bought two copies when I found it, knowing I'd keep one for myself and give the other one to Alison, my artist daughter.

Somewhere in this temporary retail space leased for the holidays, this marina of docked tables, is one table that holds books of poetry. From experience, I walk to the back and check the corner tables. Located just before the hallway that leads to the loading dock and the trash compactor, I find it.

This is where the book collector digs for Oak Island-like treasures, in the area unexplored by the less impassioned; this is where I go to find a first edition or a signed copy that has traveled the country after some bookstore shuttered its doors, a book now washed ashore and marooned on this table of poetry books. I hold my breath for a second as I arrive like a boat about to tie up to a pier.

I locate the small stacks of usual suspects. Robert Frost. Emily Dickinson. Edgar Allen Poe, though it's a collection of his stories. Anne Morrow Lindberg's *The Unicorn and Other Stories*. There's one Yeats, a Robert Penn Warren. And one hardback by someone named Raymond Carver. This name seems familiar. Haven't I read a short story of his? About some drunken couples swapping zany love stories? But this—*Where Water Comes Together with Other Water*—is a book of poetry. The 1985 hardback edition with the dust jacket is in fine condition for being moved around in the brief years since its publication. And it's long for a book of poems, easily one hundred and thirty pages, twice the length of most poetry collections. The first poem, about Carver's first job at sixteen, stocking shelves at a Woolworth's retail store, evokes the memory of my first job at that same age, stocking shelves and delivering prescriptions for a local drug store in the small Ohio coastal town of Avon Lake where I grew up. In his final poem, about fishing but not catching anything, Carver writes, "At times I felt so happy I had to quit fishing." I recall that same feeling I'd had sitting on the quarried stone piers that reached from behind the Electric Power Plant into Lake Erie, the place where I fished when I was old enough to go there alone, learning patience, and, like Carver, "listening to the sound the water made." Here is a poet writing lyrical narratives that reflect my life's experiences in ways similar to his. This experience is new to me. As a writer myself, I appreciate how his poems succeed where mine fall short, how he catches fish while I cut bait.

But it's the title poem that grabs me by my shirtfront and won't let me go. "I'm 45 years old today," Carver writes, "Would anyone believe it if I said I was once 35?" I've never encountered a poem before that addresses male midlife transition. As a man in my forties, holding this book makes me feel like I'm outside a house, looking through the window, and watching myself read or write. I stand in the Book Bazaar and read Carver's work straight through. I look back over some of the other poems, especially the ones about the water. I'm Carver's dopplegangered reader, entranced and transported.

I look across the store and through the glass windows to the parking lot outside. Cars have a layer of snow on their roofs, and large white flakes continue to fall and accumulate in the growing dark of the short winter day. I feel hungry, but I'm not sure what I'm hungry for. It's not a particular flavor or the difference between soup or sandwich. I do know that I need to eat something that will leave me feeling both full and sustained, for I have some vague task I must identify. I recall Hemingway saying that when he was hungry, he would go to the museums in Paris to look at the art, and that being hungry made him a better writer. Has reading the Carver book made me want to write? Write better? Write right now? And if I do, will I feel satiated? Is this the kind of hunger I have?

Without thinking, I set down the book and leave the store. After I brush snow off the windshield of the car while it runs and warms up, I join the traffic flow of other workers driving home.

I'm eating dinner when I wonder why I didn't buy that book of poems by Raymond Carver. What was I thinking? Did my mind just drift elsewhere in the bookstore? Nothing unusual drew my attention. Walking away from the Carver book made me feel like I'd turned and walked away from a friend of mine who was telling me about some important incident in his life and I just left in mid-sentence without even a goodbye. Am I in some way the friend himself, and is this some moment of meaning in my life and I had just walked out on myself? Perhaps something is missing, like the book itself? I need to know.

A powerful urge to hold the book in my hands and read it again, right at that moment, grips me. I feel paralyzed with embarrassment for foolishly walking away from something that held my attention so powerfully when it was in my hands. Away from it now, I feel compelled to jump up, grab my keys, and drive back to get it. The chance of the Book Bazaar still being open seems even more remote than the chance of a pop-up store having a land line to call. But even though I know this, I go anyway.

Twenty minutes later I'm standing in front of the closed store. The parking lot is empty except for my car. The

December wind is brisk and insistent, cloying its way up my pant legs and coat sleeves, down my collar. In my haste I forgot my scarf and gloves. A Cleveland Indians baseball cap I found in the car, made of cotton, offers about as much protection for my head as a handkerchief. The winter wind makes a whistling sound as it chills my exposed ears so much that they sting.

I lean close to the glass. Though the store lights are out, I can see the back corner where the small table of poetry books are dimly lit by the low wattage exit sign. No nightlight ever seemed so sad. "Hello friend," I say out loud in the direction of the table of poetry books. "I'll be back tomorrow," I say to Raymond Carver, or to the book of his poems, or to both. My cold right hand feels even colder fumbling for, then clutching the icy car keys. I turn the coat collar tighter, hunch up my shoulders, and begin my solitary walk back across the arctic expanse of the parking lot toward my car.

I'm restless, fidgety, finding it hard to get settled enough for sleep to find me. Instead, I toss and turn and tumble in a lapidary of anxiety. Closing my eyes, I make myself recall the sound water makes in creeks, rivers, beaches. The lift and lull of moving water. The rhythm of Lake Erie waves slows my breath as I enter the calm farm pond of sleep.

When the alarm goes off in the morning I wake with my head under a pillow. I call school, tell the secretary I'll be late but will get there by ten. This gives me time to stop at the Book Bazaar on my way to class.

I park the car, walk briskly across the windy expanse of the parking lot, scoot through the store's door, then move with purposeful speed toward the poetry table in the back of the store.

My joy of finding the Carver book still on the poetry table has me hyperventilating. I lift *Where Water Comes Together with Other Water* into the air as if it is a holy relic, clutch it briefly to my chest as if it is a prodigal child returned to the family. After packing it carefully for transport in my briefcase, I practically run to my car.

All day at school I obsess about the book. I have my students do in-class writing so I can reach into my desk drawer and touch the Carver book like it is a talisman. During lunch break I stay in my classroom, looking at the cover, the Marion Ettlinger author photo on the back where Carver's arms and shoulders square into a partial frame. His fiery eyes look directly into mine, his gaze is challenging, his face as serious as the honesty of the poems wrote for this book.

The back of the book jacket is like a mirror in which I see myself. I recognize in the reflection my own immediate need as a writer to find the honesty to write this phase of my life. The challenge is clear. I breathe deep, exhale slowly, and accept finding myself living a moment where one poet's writing comes together with another poet's writing.

Outside, the shadows of parked cars and bare winter trees grow longer across the parking lot and lawns of snow. Inside and seated at my faculty office desk, I feel alive in a way that allows me to fully experience this moment. Though I feel connected to another person, to another writer who I've met through a book, writing with common purpose, still I lack a vocabulary to express it.

Then something Carver writes in one of his poems comes to mind: "If this sounds like the story of a life, okay." It's as if he's telling me not to define or dissect or deconstruct everything. As if he's telling me that sometimes its best just to trust the way the story sounds, which is sometimes enough, even if I can't find the word to say it aloud.

I realize the book I've acquired has given me more than I have bargained for. It is going to connect with my life each time I read it again, finding in successive readings not what is new in the book, but what I keep discovering about myself in each subsequent rereading. It's like when I was fifteen and read *Catcher in the Rye* for the first time, a book that traveled with me to college and beyond. Little is as profound as the gift of finding the right book at a significant time in one's life. If *Catcher in the Rye* was the book of my adolescence opening into my early adulthood, will *Where Water Comes Together with Other Water* be the book of my middle life transition? And why not? Caver's story is my story, too.

Looking up from my faculty desk, I return my gaze to the wintery landscape outside my window.

The shortest day of the year is nearly here. Change is coming. In incremental turns, the days will slowly grow longer, brighter, warmer. Snow will become sleet, sleet will become rain, and rain will bring another spring.

A sense of movement bears me along. I will merge into this moment of my life with a newly arriving stage. I will trust the flow of this new current.

# Three

*You adulterate the truth as you write. There isn't any pretense that you try to arrive at the literal truth. And the only consolation when you confess to this flaw is that you are seeking to arrive at poetic truth.*
–W.G. Sebald

# Refractions

The moon is eating the sun. I close my left eye and look with the open right one through a dark bottle of Great Lakes Brewery Edmund Fitzgerald Porter at the afternoon sky. If the sun were not as diminished as industrial objects rusting in the Midwest, the eclipse would be almost total. It's as dim as dusk at 2:30 in the afternoon. The air is absolutely still.

My brother in law Adam is filming the event partly because he's a videographer and filmmaker and partly because he has video camera lenses dark as a welder's visor he's using to view the blacking hole moving across the sun. As he leaves and goes into the garage, he says the moon looks like it has collapsed into a crescent.

Adam returns with two sturdy cardboard boxes. Uses his Swiss Army knife to cut a small hole in each of the boxes. He hands my wife Molly and me the boxes, and one by one we each put them on. Our breathing amplifies, fractures into a trio of sound waves against the hammer, anvil, and stirrup that form the audio grotto of our ears.

Turning the hole toward the sun, we spin around to examine the flat brown cardboard where a tiny partial moon is revealed. We've captured a circle inside a square. But it's upside down and backward, the way an image is inside an eyeball. I could be inside a camera, taking a picture of a solar eclipse. I blink like a shutter and click: the image locks into my memory.

I imagine a small album of photographs my wife would take of us out there in the yard. Photo: two people dorky as adolescents, dressed as robots in the false dusk. Photo: a square metallic robot's face with a small rectangular camera operating from one eye socket.

With the cardboard box removed, I close my eyes and see stringy floaters first, then small dark stars, then a constellation of tiny dots seemingly projected on the inside of my right eyelid. They look like ants crawling on a glass window. Like spring tree pollen. Like the small dusting of rust that remains on the driveway where an old car is parked. Or like the kind of particulate matter emitted from a coal fired power plant and congregating on a car's hood, windshield, top, or trunk.

At the eye exam, the dark-haired ophthalmologist whispers in the outside hallway to her redheaded assistant who holds her palm to her lips. They shake their heads in unison, lean their heads in toward each other. Their serious faces return to the room where I wait in the ophthalmic exam reclining chair. Immediate surgery is necessary; my right eye will be drained and inflated with gas.

What I thought was my cataract returning like an unwanted prodigal is instead the sudden arrival of an EMS vehicle, round red lights flashing like a detaching retina.

I recall a helium balloon from a childhood summer carnival. Untied from my wrist, it rose and floated up to where the ceiling met the wall, holding there as if attached by glue. I fell asleep watching it.

When I woke, the balloon had grown slack, semi-deflated, and saggy, hovering about a foot above the floor, its string like a disconnected spider thread attached to a small black shadow on the floor. My moon had collapsed to a crescent. The top was now on the bottom, the bottom on top: two flipped geometric figures.

Photo: Cyclops pursuing Ulysses. New photo: the epicurean one-eyed writer Jim Harrison eating oysters. Another photo: the young poet Robert Creeley, his black eye patch matching a shoulder-perched crow. Another: you opening your front door next Halloween to find me trick-or-treating. I'm the one dressed as a cardboard robot holding a helium balloon.

# Audio Echo

The only known recording of Virginia Woolf reading her work aloud is from a 1937 BBC Radio broadcast. The graininess of the audio is in the recorder, not the reader. I know Woolf by her prose, by fading images from book covers. Her monaural voice, though unfamiliar, does not seem surprising. Elegant, carefully cadenced, upper class Bloomsbury British. Have I always heard her sound this way, in my head, as I imagined Clarissa Dalloway would sound when speaking?

Woolf's recorded talk is titled "Craftsmanship," but in actuality she is telling a story about the story of words. Their histories, preferences. About why writers ask them to dance in their sentences. How words hate making money. Or being lectured about in public. I'm not certain I agree with her when she says words hate being useful.

Outside the window is another snowy northeast Ohio afternoon. The monochromatic scene outdoors reminds me of black and white photographs from the nineteenth through the mid-twentieth century. Flakes fall at a rate quite perfectly comparable to the pace at which Woolf speaks in the recording.

Four crows hop and flap around on the slanted roof of the house across the alley. On the thin branches of a huge maple tree in the yard, three more balance, rising and falling with the gust and pitch of the wind. These birds could be four dancers with three more waiting in the wings to join them on stage. Or paper puppets in an old Eastern European tradition. They could be letters at play, forming words, reconfiguring into variations on themselves. Seven crows in a snowy landscape.

The dark birds rise together in flight, a sporadic flocking, as they disappear from the frame of my small window. I imagine this is how lead type might tumble after use from a letterpress case in a print shop. How window is type case is window. How words spill easily off a tongue and out of the mouth. This wintery afternoon has a graininess about it, a suffused texture, as if from an old album of fading photographs.

I search for a useful word that might give voice to a blue feeling or a dark thought, but no words take flight from my tongue. By now the crows have flown into the distance but still I hear their raucous cawing. A raspy haunted sort of sound, as if from an ancient time. A monaural song crafted from useful words sounding, echoing, evolving toward stereo.

# A Brief Meditation on Color

Nobel Poet Czeslaw Milosz's "A Little Treatise on Colors" from his 1997 collection *Road-side Dog* reminds me of Helen Frankenthaler's bright 1971 painting "Humming Gold" which hangs in the Cleveland Museum of Art. I sense, both in reading and in viewing, the struggle on the part of artists to make color come across to the reader, the viewer.

Milosz muses, "Why this excessive poverty of language any time we deal with colors? What do we have at our disposal when we try to name the splendor of colors?" The poet's eye sees more hue than his word-hoard holds, so that, for Milosz, he has "encountered difficulty in describing autumn in the valley of the Connecticut River in a precise and simple manner, without the props of comparison and metaphor." That latter phrase holds the key: the poet's gift of figurative language fails when it comes to color; color—precise and simple and intuitive—is the painter's realm.

Helen Frankenthaler demonstrates this in her 1971 painting "Humming Gold." Amazing gold-yellows overwhelm the viewer, balanced with muted blue and green blocks, small dark line of contrast, of division, of distinction, and one white spot, unpainted, another kind of contrast: so precise and simple to show off this specific gold. And yet, that white spot looks vaguely like a leg, as if the painter can picture the metaphorical prop which the poet finds failing him.

I know the paucity and limits of language. My whole life I have tried to describe the color of Ohio lakes and rivers and creeks, of its morning sky, cascading and dynamic cloud banks, and the brilliant visual jewelry of its Lake Erie sunsets and sunrises.

# Thank You Card

Dear Genevieve, Dear Jeanne, Dear Mother, Dear Mom:
I've been meaning to call, trying to call, thinking of calling,
wanting to call you. But the phone rings and rings. But
the voice mail isn't working. But the cell phone has been
cancelled. But there is a new phone in your old room in the
assisted living facility. I think of writing you a letter, sending
you a notecard, penning you a postcard. You'd like that, for
you were from one of the last generations of letter writers.
But I don't know what address to send to. But I don't have
any of those Forever postage stamps. I wanted to tell you
about what I've been doing, how Ali and Mike are doing, that
Ross and Ashlie brought your two newest great-grandsons
into the world, how they are all here in Ohio now, how good
family feels. You would know.

I miss hearing about the small details of your day, how you
still dislike the toast at breakfast, how you walked a couple
of doorways down the hallway without your walker, how
you heard from Ken and Cher, your telling me again about
the day Ken took you to the park near where you lived when
he visited you in Florida, how he pushed you on a swing.
About how good Dick and Linda are to you, always there,
always there. I miss knowing you are still with us, back here
in Ohio, the heartland, your heart the hearth the family
gathered around. But that is past. But that is always. But love

is longer than ninety years, larger than all time. But love is a poppy seed that grows in our hearts, becoming a red flower in our chests that neither wilts nor falters.

Today I am filled with memories. How you always said your father was a handsome man. How you loved your brothers, your sister Ruth who you, the good sister, always cared for. How you told me that you often missed your mother. I remember myself home sick from school, watching old black and white movies on the TV with you, remember myself as a child whose any hurt you healed, remember how you were always the candle in the long night. But now the votive has used its wax to light the darkness for you. But still the wick remains.

Dear Genevieve, Dear Jeanne, Dear Mother, Dear Mom: I am thinking of you right now, in Florida again, all three of your sons and their wives visiting the place where your ashes and Dad's ashes are interred. I recall the small paper valentine that Dad gave you in high school, the one you always had held in place between mirror and frame in your room. I imagine how each time you viewed it, the creased paper of your aged skin turned to ironed linen as you saw your sixteen-year-old-self looking back, blushing with young love as a red poppy bloomed in your heart.

# My Father's Watch

Leaves from the gnarled apple tree fell, then were blown to the west. One late apple dropped, not fast, not like physics, but with a movement as incrementally and achingly slow as terminal cancer spreads. Yet its contact with the ground was sudden, like the impact of
a doctor's sad last diagnosis. The apple stopped moving. Bees flew back toward the hive. Orchards grew as silent as are rooms after the last drawn breath leaves the body.

My older brother holds my grandfather's antique pocket watch, but I don't want that. Instead, I take a pair of cufflinks of Irish setters my father rarely wore, then pick up his Swiss Longines wristwatch. I lay the fifty-year-old time piece across my palm as if it's a bird, a medal, or a bird-medal. I carefully pull out the thin stem, turning it gently back and forth, winding it as if I am reviving some endangered fledgling. It ticks, tocks, and keeps time, the cadence of a comforting heart. Isn't it time I brought it back to life? So little time has passed since I saw my father, his face as serious as a clock's, and which I tried to read while his life was winding down. Though I wind this memory like a watch, nothing is revived. Yet my uncomforted heart ticks mechanically on.

I carry a bottle of beer and a glass out to the screened porch. I sit on the top step, peer among the birch trees for buds. The neighbor's radio is playing old songs—big band music, Benny Goodman, or the Dorsey Brothers, the soundtrack for my father's life. The times I would come over with my own children to see him, we would sit on his porch, watch the kids climb his apple tree, and drink cold, sweet beer as we eased into August afternoons. When he was dying, states away in Florida, betrayed by his body, I drove down to be with him. *What did you bring me?* he asked, his eyes round as fruit, his arms thin as weathered tree branches. But my mouth sat dumb in my face. But my empty hands lay in my lap like fallen apples.

A poem by Li-Young Lee comes to mind. In the orchard, he sees a shovel and mistakes it for his deceased father. He recalls his father showing him a wasp buzzing in the juice of an over-ripe pear, the feeling of fullness instead of emptiness. Hearing the radio play, listening to Lester Brown, Artie Shaw, and Paul Whiteman, I understand. Then I go back inside, bring out a second glass. I pour a bottle of beer into a glass, set it down for my dad. Even as I welcome the company of his memory, still I bargain with loss.

# Off the Cuff

John Joseph Miltner gets dressed to go to the wedding. Today his son Frank will marry Ethel Crowe, his fiancée from a good Irish Catholic family. John takes his linen shirt from a hanger and buttons the starched white collar onto the shirt, one button on the back of the neck, one each on either side of the top front button. John removes the dress shirt from the hanger, puts it on, and buttons it from the bottom up to the top, where in a few minutes he'll stand in front of a mirror in order to tie a four-in-hand knot for the short mutely-colored striped silk necktie that will match his black six button double breasted suit coat. But first, he will clip the cuffs of his sleeves together. On a regular day, he would use double clam shell buttons, one each on either side of the buttonhole. But today is not a regular day. Today he will dress "to the nines" and wear his octagonal gold cufflinks with the small diamonds. Such cufflinks announce to the world that he is a successful man, one who also owns a gold watch that sits snuggly in the pocket of his vest. He folds and doubles each of his long shirt cuffs, then inserts the curved stems of his gold links to hold the cuffs together. Before he leaves the room, he adjusts his silk tie, puts on his double-breasted coat, and buttons it close to his middle-aged body. John looks at his reflection in the mirror, checks that the sleeve peeks out from his cuff enough so that light from the wooden double hung window can catch the sun in the diamond links of his French cuffs.

Frank Leon Miltner looks for his favorite stick pin inside a small mortised wooden box in his dresser drawer. His fingers move his father's gold pocket watch. He looks among the stick pins, notes the lacy and intricate pattern of one, the polished oyster shell glean of another, then selects the one he's had a jeweler make for him, the one that is made from his father's lone cufflink that he'd saved. The cufflink was once part of a pair, but his father, John, lost the other one. His father never told him how it happened. Frank imagines his father catching his cufflink on the exit door of the Lorain electric trolley one hurried Sunday morning on his way to mass at Saint Ignatius church. He probably wouldn't have even felt it catch, break, and fall in two loose pieces. His father may have felt instead how the cuff flapped loose, like an old man whose dentures had fallen out and gotten lost. Frank likes to wear the stick pin high on the tie so that it sits in the middle of the chevron when he buttons his suit coat. It reminds Frank of his father who wore his best cufflinks to the church on the day of his wedding day to Ethel. Today he wears it to the church where his middle son, Eugene, home from the war in the Pacific now, will marry his fiancée, Genevieve Higgins, who is from a good Irish Catholic family, and who likes to be called Jeanne. Frank studies his reflection in the bedroom mirror, then turns a bit until the lamplight catches the diamond stickpin and makes it sparkle. He goes downstairs where Ethel waits for him, then they get in the Chevrolet coupe, a General Motors car like the ones he makes at the Brookpark Plant, and drives Ethel and himself to Saint Ignatius church for the wedding.

Gene Miltner wears a new dark blue worsted wool suit he bought at Higbee's department store. Gene likes the feel of a well-fitting fashionable suit worn with a sharp stylish tie. A salesman first of steel bolts, he wears the suit with the pride of the army uniform he wore home from the war, his Midwestern skin tanned from the Hawaiian sun. Standing in front of the full-length mirror in the upstairs of the split-level house, he buttons the front of his white polyester wash and wear dress shirt with the French cuffs and sleeve placket button, then adds and Windsor knots a polyester striped tie. He finishes getting dressed for the wedding by adding a pair of faux-gold Swank cufflinks and a matching tie tack from his top dresser drawer. While lifting out the tie tack, Gene sees the stickpin his father, Frank, made from the remaining one of the set of his Grandpa John's cufflink. He wonders about reworking it into a decorative ring to wear on his right ring hand opposite his gold wedding band, the possibility of remounting the gold square with a small diamond in its center on to a wide gold band. A ring that would remind him of both his father and his Grandpa John. A ring to wear on his hand that would connect him to his family past, to the Ohio Miltner men that have preceded him. Finally, he adds the gold Longines watch his brother-in-law Joe Higgins gave him after his discharge in the late forties from the navy. He admires its thin gold face, feels the soft leather band. Gene looks at himself in the mirror, likes how the outfit looks complete. He's now ready to drive his wife, Jeanne, in his company car, to the wedding of his middle son, Bob, to Linda Smith, the last of his three sons to marry.

On the day of my son Ross's wedding to Ashlie Sullivan, from a local Irish family, I put on a black tuxedo as Ross has requested me to do. I haven't worn one since my senior prom, and this time it feels appropriate because I am the father of the groom. I add a black pressed wool felt pork pie hat to match the black cloche hat my girlfriend Molly wears to accompany her black dress, one with a white front and a vertical row of black buttons. On my left wrist is my father's watch. On my left ring finger is my father's ring, the one made from his grandfather's cufflink by way of his father's stick pin. The ring was given to me by my mother after my father passed away. I wear it to my son's wedding in memory of his grandfather. The ring is loose on my finger, which is smaller than my father's was. Dancing at the reception with Molly and my family members, the ring sparkles under the disco ball that the DJ brought. Still, I'm cautious on the dance floor, concerned that if I'm not careful, I might lose it.

The first time I marry Molly we elope on an impulse. When the city clerical workers who provided the marriage license asks when we plan to do our vows, Molly answers it will possibly be in the afternoon, depending if we get a return call. We all share a hearty laugh. A few hours later, we are at the Wedding Chapel, on Cleveland Avenue in Canton, Ohio, located behind El Campesino Mexican Restaurant. I wear blue jeans and a dark blue Mexican shirt and Molly wears a black wrap dress with small white polka dots. The person who performs the ceremony is a seemingly seven-foot woman in a black cassock who hands Molly some paper flowers to use in the under four-minute ceremony. The taped music she plays sounds like a techno rendition of Enya. Molly places my father's ring on my finger at the ceremony as my wedding ring, and I place her great aunt Betsy's white gold band next to the matching diamond engagement ring on her finger. My ring feels loose and hers feels tight. When Molly told Betsy she'd used the ring, Betsy told her to keep the rings since she wasn't planning to use them again. After the ceremony, we call our families on our cell phones and tell them we eloped and married. We drive to Lucca's in downtown Canton where we eat our usual favorites, chicken piccata and rare steak. We take home a whole lemon cake to share while sitting on our screened-in porch.

The second time Molly and I marry, the following July, is a family and friends ceremony under enormous oak trees in her parents' shaded yard. The vows are the ones we've written for ourselves. Our close friend Shannon Young, who presides in a red dress, is the focal point of the ceremony. Molly wears a white dress and a large white summer hat, and I don blue silk pants, a white linen shirt with blue stripes, and a double-breasted white silk blazer, all carefully selected from area thrift stores and picked up the day before from the dry cleaners. We use the same rings, her great aunt Betsy's and my father's. This is much more a celebration than a ceremony, and we all feel as joyous as only days in midsummer in Ohio can. The diamonds in our rings sparkle in the sunshine.

I return from a local vintage jeweler and appraiser who has sized my father's ring to my left finger, opposite the same one on which he wore the ring when he was alive. For him, it was second to his wedding band to my mother, but for me, it is both wedding band and my family heritage ring. I will only remove it to play steel slide guitar on my Fender Stratocaster, something I learned to do before the ring was sized, and after tendonitis kept me from chording and playing the way I learned to do when I was fifteen.

After the time I eventually pass from this life, the ring will go to my son, Ross, who can size it to fit his hand, reaching back and connecting himself with the Ohio Miltner men in his family. And when Ross passes, the ring will pass on to one of his two sons, my grandsons, Jackson or Evan, one of whom will put on the ring that goes back to his father Ross, his grandfather Robert, his great grandfather Gene, his great, great grandfather Frank, and his great, great, great grandfather John who saved an orphaned diamond cufflink. How could Grandpa John have imagined the value it might have someday, or what it could come to mean to his family line six generations after? For who knows what small fragment of a life once lived might become a token, a talisman, a touchstone for the telling of tales about a family's history, its potential outcomes, or unforeseeable futures.

# A Cinemagical Film Festival

Picture a west sider driving from Avon Lake, Bay Village, Westlake, Rocky River, or Lakewood to get to Public Square in downtown Cleveland. Image how, whether taking the I-490 highway to Ontario Street, Clifton Avenue over the Main Avenue Bridge, or the Detroit-Superior Bridge, they arrive at the base of the fifty-two-story 1930s Terminal Tower which is, like a lighthouse, the visual marker that guides drivers to the city center. See the drivers travel along West Huron road to the Tower City Complex situated on a cliff that overlooks the Flats of the Cuyahoga River below.

Formed 13,000 years ago, the Cuyahoga, a Mohawk name meaning "crooked (or winding) river," begins in Geauga County, in northeast Ohio, east of Cleveland, where the east and west branches of the river join in rural Burton to become the Cuyahoga River. Continuing through the Cuyahoga Valley National Park, the river passes the Standing Rock in Kent, and winds through the industrial valley down to the Flats and then on to the river's mouth at Whiskey Island. The Flats are known to west side Irish descendants as the place where their unwanted immigrant ancestors were sent to die of typhus.

My Crowe and Higgins ancestors, from Counties Clare and Mayo in the west of Ireland, were evicted and displaced from their homes by absentee English landlords, left to working for half a meal to feed a whole family. Following the economic and cultural devastation of the Great Hunger that resulted from the potato famine, many indentured themselves for a ticket to America.

If there were documentary films then, or smart phone video recorders, my great-grandfather James Higgins would be seen as a twelve-year-old arriving in the new homeland, just released from steerage, his young foot on the bow of a wooden ship docking in New York Harbor. Later he'd be seen running away from his cruel uncle in Philadelphia who beat him. A grainy scene of him slipping away to become a cabin boy, starting on boats then moored on the Cuyahoga or the shipping piers in Cleveland. By the finale of the film, he'd be shown ending his career as captain of a ship making pleasure trips from the 9th Street Pier to Buffalo or Detroit and back. One of those returns, as my mother told the story, was in 1916 when he captained his ship from Buffalo back to Cleveland during the Black Friday storm on Lake Erie that claimed half a dozen ships and nearly fifty lives. Lightning illuminates him like a flash bulb, capturing an image of him in his dark woolen sweater and double-breasted peacoat, his captain's cap, and his great, dark beard hiding the mouth that clutches his white clay pipe. The camera catches his fierce look, shows his hands grasping the ship's wheel while facing the storm. A panorama displays a tableau of anxious families and friends cheering as he brings his ship with all his passengers and crew, finding safe harbor as his ship is docked on a night that claimed the lives of so many others.

From Huron Road, I look down at the Flats of the Cuyahoga River. In another block I'll turn down to a parking lot closer to the riverbank that leads me to the parking garage under the Tower City Complex of the Terminal Tower. After

I park, I walk to the underground entrance to the Cleveland International Film Festival.

In 1977, as urban movie houses were closing and movies began playing more regularly at malls, the Cedar Lee Theater in Cleveland Heights—which showed "foreign films," that is, British, subtitled, or "blue" French films—launched the first Cleveland International Film Festival, or CIFF, by showing eight films over as many weeks. No records seem to have been kept—it was, after all, an idea conceived of in the moment, not with some sense of eventual artistic or historic importance—but it was enough of a success to hold the CIFF again in 1978. The program grew and in 1991 the festival was moved to the eleven-plex theater at Tower City in downtown Cleveland, a complex that includes hotels, shopping, restaurants, and public transportation: busses, the Rapid Transit and the Shaker Rapid line. CIFF has become the largest film festival in Ohio, boasting hundreds of short and feature-length films from nearly 70 different countries including Haiti, Barbados, the Maldives, Kazakhstan, Venezuela, Rwanda, Jordan, Iraq, Albania, Tanzania, and Cuba; but that is what makes the festival international, a cultural exchange via the screen, the sights and sounds and stories from other countries. And this exchange has grown in popularity. By 2012, the CIFF saw its *one millionth* attendee at the festival, with an audience of some 85,000 attendees over eleven days. That's like filling the Browns Stadium plus the playing field, or Progressive Stadium twice for the Indians, or the Quicken Loans Arena four times for the Cavaliers. That's more people than live in Lorain or Youngstown. That's the number of people in Parma, Ohio, or Lincoln, Nebraska. And it takes a lot to put on a film festival that long for that many people—partnerships with well over 200 non-profits, arts councils, media groups and corporate sponsors, plus hundreds of volunteers. That's not so difficult—Cleveland, after all, is the second largest city in the state.

For about 20 yards or so, couples and groups of three or four range along the long hallway, some talking, most looking around. They wear spring or winter coats, a few hats. There's a spattering of backpacks. A few hold bottles of water, some hold bags of popcorn. A line forms behind a purple cardboard sign on a small stand that lists the name of the film soon to be shown. The guy holding the sign has his Volunteer tag on. He looks at the line and checks the time on his smart phone.

A small domestic drama plays out in the line in front of me. A couple are going through their pockets, as rapid and methodical as people scratching ants at a picnic. "Don't you have them?" the middle-aged woman asks, her hand in her handbag. "I thought you did," says the guy with the graying ponytail, unzipping pockets in his North Face jacket. I put my hand over my heart, over the inside pocket of my leather coat with the ticket I picked up from Will Call, with my stamped Free Parking tag. The Volunteer calls down the line, turning his sign around in slow circles, "We're leaving, everyone." Then as briskly as schoolchildren heading out to recess, we follow to see a film called *Detropia*.

Not many rush to see a documentary about Detroit, generally viewed as one of the economically hardest hit cities in the country and the origin of the American rustbelt and visual source for "ruin photography" or "ruin porn." Once the major auto production city in the world, the "Motor City," "Motown" Detroit has seen the majority of its auto manufacturing jobs outsourced to China and Mexico. The film follows the story lines of people as diverse as an auto union official, the owner of a local bar, a blogger who works at a coffee shop, and the mayor of a city that is bankrupt. How could it not be? After peaking at 1.8 million residents in 1950, an emblem of the triumph of the middle class, the city is down to 700,000 residents living in an area the size of Manhattan, Boston, and San Francisco put together, but with 90,000 vacant houses and an unofficial unemployment rate of nearly 50%. The popcorn becomes harder to swallow as the movie raises endless questions about the future of the city, the Midwest, and the country as a whole. Yet it offers no answers. Decay porn images of abandoned buildings and blocks cleared of houses haunt the screen the way apocalypse films do, only those lurching down the streets are not zombies, just people struggling to survive in a city where even hope seems about to be foreclosed upon.

Detroit is struggling, but it's trying. It's giving empty houses away for free, and artists are coming from as far away as Germany to move in. Deer and pheasants have returned to the abandoned neighborhoods, living among the tall grasses in a city where their sports teams are called Lions and Tigers. In my head, I hear an old Motown song, from the days when Detroit was America's music capital: "Tell it like it is . . ." And *Detropia* does just that. It is a brave film, a difficult film, a necessary film. This documentary has no car chases, no dancing, no bailing out by George Bailey.

As the end credits roll, the audience begins to clap, as I do, for the bravery of making this important film. I believe we really clap for what art does—courageously presenting difficult, sobering, yet necessary truths. No matter how impactful a film can be, how much its message clings to us like a shadow, still I leave the dark theater alone. As I exit out into the night, I feel drawn by the pull of the downtown lights that lead me on, seeking the company of others to abate my momentary sense of isolation.

Flannery's Irish Pub at East Fourth and Prospect is close enough both to Tower City Cinema and Public Square to stop in for a sandwich and a heady Guinness draft, a shot of Jamison's, or both. Great Lakes Brewery would have been good too, a local business worthy of support, but it's on the other side of the Cuyahoga river. Flannery's evokes the old Irish bars in Cleveland, like the working class neighborhood bar my uncle Bob the cop had on the near west side when I was a kid, and where my Dad worked on busy weekends to help him out. Flannery's still rings a bell for last call, and will set up a draft or a shot along the bar for you, as long as you order under the wire and pay the tab.

While I'm nursing an Imperial pint of Guinness I keep thinking about Detroit, out on the Western basin of Lake Erie, about how empty the islands are, how deserted houses in a city can be. Yet hope still lives in Detroit, as alive as the Depression era Detroit Industry Murals painted by Diego Rivera in which Ford auto workers stare proudly back at viewers, unblinking and stoic, as committed as current workers at the electric power company are to keeping the darkness at bay.

As I look out the windows of Flannery's at the city lights, I see the bright downtown in this city where I was born. Thousands of people come downtown to see these CIFF films, support the local economy, stay at the Ritz-Carlton, the Radisson, the Wyndham. Cleveland is still hanging in, tough as those Irish boyos who came up from the Flats to become policemen and firemen and politicians and ships' captains. The bar is alive: full, loud, raucous with talk and laughter.

On the TV above the bar, the Ohio State Buckeyes, up by four points over the Kansas Jayhawks, are on a good scoring drive. The final buzzer sounds as the Buckeyes win. Everyone in Flannery's claps and cheers as more drafts are poured and set out on the bar. On nights like this, we can all feel like we're winners.

# Hard Shale Dreams

The North Coast at Avon Point isn't merely a binary of inland sea and sky, or lake and land. It's a Great Lakes coastline is defined by high shale cliffs. Hard as consonants, sharp, gray shale usurps the soft earth and loam. Waves curl, round as vowels where Ohio begins its land's end tumble of stones. Sitting on a wooden bench on the bluff at Mayor's Park, I watch as the world within my vision fragments into a triad. In the distance the horizon would begin its long division: below, lake; above, sky; between, shore. No wonder I think in threes. If a flashing bolt suddenly cracks the sky, I imagine an electric string simultaneously tying together a quartet of earth, water, sky, and fire.

Atop the shale bluff near Mayor's Park, a willow tree, worn down from ice and winter winds from the northwest, leans back from the cliff at an angle that dares to resist the pull of gravity. Above it, sea gulls bicker like quarrelsome siblings. A lone crow caws from its perch at the top of the leaning willow. The crow faces the lake. Something on the surface of the water has caught its attention. It could be a mallard duck, a piece of driftwood, or a dead walleye the crow will eat when the waves wash it ashore on the small stone beach.

Located on the Avon Point bluff, alongside the old Lake Road that runs from Cleveland to Lorain, is Lake Shore Cemetery. It dates back to the late 1800s when the first settlers arrived to cut the great oaks and maples, to plow flat the historic raised Indian mounds, to plant Concord grape vineyards and apple orchards. Like many things begun with small intention, much of the early history is lore or lost. Historical documents record births and deaths, but not the minds of the settlers who first settled upon the idea that this particular one-acre plot of land would be used as a community burial ground. Or why the first grave was dug in hard shale on a bluff rather than a mile or so inland in the tillable earth where shovel and plow could turn the topsoil.

History is like dropped shale: layered rock that shatters, exposing fragments of sediment to sunlight. Yet only a curious few try to undertake the painstaking process of reconstructing the parts again into a knowable whole. Instead, local memory, oral history, and conjecture combine into versions rather than explanations, like blank pages encountered periodically while reading chronicles of the past, so that some parts of the puzzle remain unfindable.

Unmarked slabs of sandstone mark several of the graves at Lake Shore Cemetery. Those interred there remain unknown. The names of some have been erased by the force of weather on soft stone overgrown with blue-green lichen. The names of others were never known. Perhaps the first graves were dug for a French trapper or a Native American who traveled along the old Indian lakeside trail, yet no makers survive by way of support for such suppositions.

The first two known interred were Pennsylvanian militia who died during the 1813 Battle of Lake Erie and washed ashore. Others were fishermen or sailors who drowned when caught surprised by unexpected storms. An eighth of the average depth of Lake Superior, a fifth of Lakes Ontario and

Michigan, and only a third of Huron, Erie is the shallowest of the Great Lakes. At barely sixty feet deep on average, Erie kicks up quickly, turning the whitecaps of the waves into what looks like a chaotic eruption of saw blades. Water washes over bulwarks before a man can call for help. Water rushes into mouths and lungs before a man can scream, his eyes the washed-out color of lake water roughed up to whitecaps. Several of the shale or granite grave markers of the anonymous sailors, toppled over the years from settling and shifting, are the presumed sites that mark where these nameless sailors were first laid down for their long sleep.

Buckeye trees stand in a sentry row along the graveyard's western side. Each autumn the trees drop shiny dark nuts that look like the eyes of buck deer. Fallen to the ground, they look like the lost eyes of the dead. Some of the names remaining on the oldest marked graves are the same names given to streets that used to be boundary roads of early orchard and vineyard owners. The history of community families whose names mark the current roads— Duff, Curtis, Beck, Moore, Tomanek, Jaycox—have been buried under layers of new developments, small malls, commerce, and splashes of advertising. What's contemporary on the top layers are images which belie the ideas of the past which are encased in the layers below.

There's more than mortality at stake, or the value of history as a field of study. It's about how history gets read. Commercial sites tell only the story of what is to be sold, while historical sites can be about how the story is told. Walking observantly through an old resting place and thoughtfully viewing the stone markers is akin to reading a book, to reading stones as pages that introduce the visitor-reader to previous local generations. American playwrights Edgar Lee Masters, who staged the cemetery of Spoon River in 1915 with each gravestone as a narrative poem, and Thornton Wilder, who took his audiences to Grover's Corners in 1938 as a theatrical drama, both understood that cemeteries were metaphorically works of literature. Lake Shore Cemetery at Avon Point is an historical tome of my hometown, connecting me back to its first settlers. At times when I am returning to or passing through Avon Lake, I'll stop, walk the lanes of the old cemetery, as if re-reading one of my favorite books, noting how while the site itself remains unchanged, I recognize in my musing how it is I myself who continues to grow and change.

The fathers and brothers and sons and neighbors who moved within sight or sound of this lake did so to live close to Erie. They looked daily through windows for a glass-flat lake surface to mirror their hard shale dreams of what spinner or new lure to use to troll for walleye or yellow perch or white bass. They practiced patience before the crow called them in to dock at piers that are the shape and color of toppled gravestones. Their names will follow their corporeal existence as seasons of weather erase them from stone, from history, from memory. Eventually my words will fade, reduced to undecipherable runes scratched into stone like the figures of bison or deer rendered on cave walls, prescient and ritualistic, yet meaningless beyond conjecture. Regardless of origin or time or intent, the message is always the same: someone from the past is trying to speak of the living, the dead, the soon to pass, of the next about to be born.

# Ferry Crossing

An expanding ring in the water of the bay shows where the coot upended and plunged into the Strait of Juan de Fuca. I'd count the seconds except I know how calibration and enumeration poke holes in magic. The water bird doesn't come up for air.

On the bow of the Port Angeles to Victoria ferry, a woman stands, leaning her face into the light rain, pushing herself into the blue-gray moment. While I watch through the window, I can see that for her, experiences are about the senses, about some need to feel the leaving of one place for some new one. For me, docking in an unfamiliar bay, wandering the streets of a town new to me fills me with wonder and promise.

In the dark of the motel room I wake to the sound of seagulls on Washington's north coast. I sense the saltwater is a hundred yards away, intuit its inevitable rise and change, and feel the momentary serenity from knowing that. I remember what I learned growing up along Ohio's north coast: on the other side of that water is another country.

I ride the ferry from the bow, aviator sunglasses like silver dollars over my eyes. It's good to squint into the wind and not feel it like a cold hand on my back. Better to kick against the breathtaking current that wants to pull down. Best, like the coot, to be patient. Then come up for air.

# Black River Bridge

Low rain clouds blockade your mouth, Black River, where the slow ore boats used to call port on the Lake Erie coastline. The lighthouse is an artifact, the shipyard shut down, the steel mills idle. You are not a highway exit to a mall. Your high school sports teams lose regularly to athletes from the barrens of Elyria, Amherst, or Norwalk. Below the old Erie Avenue lift bridge, fishermen toss tumorous catfish up on the bank, dinner for river rats and stray cats. As I cross over your rickety, rutted, and rusty steel structure, the sound of my car's tires hums like a swarm of angry yellow jackets, their stingers like sharpened hail or dull iron nails falling from an endless iron-gray sky.

You ruined old river, sleeping under junk mail and political advertising in the doorways of boarded up buildings on run-down Broadway, what is to become of you? All your former lovers—steel, automotive, shipbuilding—have left town looking for work. They'd send you love letters filled with promises of return, sanctuary, or salvation, but your mailbox is rusted shut, but your address is erased. Poor Black River, you lonely stepsister in this sad fairy tale of Ohio rivers. Nowhere near as lovely as the Vermillion, Sandusky, Maumee, or Auglaize, you languish from neglect and the scars of continued economic decimation. No one, lost river of industry, dark river of my youth, kisses your mouth each night along your shale and sand shoreline. It is in the graffiti tattoos and hard shadows under your bridges that your story is written. Yet in the doorway of a boarded-up building, huddled in darkness against a storm, a young couple press together, like flint striking to make sparks.

# Notes

1. The Alex Preston epigram is from his review of *Outpost* by Dan Richards (*The Guardian*, 8 April 2019).
2. "Double Exposure" is in response to an untitled print by Rachel Beamer.
3. "Shadows of Crows Crossing Over" is for Caroline Messmer Higgins.
4. "Tasting a New Moon" is for Molly Fuller.
5. The Matsuo Bashō epigram is from *The Essential Haiku: Versions of Bashō, Buson, and Issa,* translated and edited by Robert Hass (Ecco Press, 1995).
6. "Out of Alsace" is for Genevieve Alice Higgins Miltner.
7. "Desperados" is for Glenn Frey.
8. "Death of the Fugitive Charles Floyd" is inspired by the photograph *Alley, East Liverpool, Ohio* by Andrew Borowiec.
9. "A Brief Meditation on Color" is in response to an essay by Czeslaw Milosz.
10. The W.G. Sebald epigram is from *The Emergence of Memory: Conversations with W.G. Sebald,* edited by Lynne Sharon Schwartz (Seven Stories Press, 2010).
11. "Audio Echoes" is for Virginia Woolf.
12. "Thank You Card" is for Genevieve Alice Higgins Miltner.
13. "My Father's Watch" is for Eugene Charles Miltner.
14. "Off the Cuff" is for Jackson and Evan Miltner.

# Acknowledgments

Thanks to the editors of the following journals and presses in which these pieces, sometimes in different forms or with other titles, first appeared:

*Being Home: An Essay Anthology* (Madville Publishing), "Into the Bargain."

*Boom Project: Voices of a Generation Anthology* (Butler Books), "Tasting A New Moon"

*Buried Letter*, "A Cinemagical Film Festival," "Out of Alsace," and "Quiet"

*Del Sol Review*, "Refractions"

*DIAGRAM*, "The Valdemar Car"

*Eastern Iowa Review*, "Audio Echo"

*Forbidden Peak Press*, "Swift Current of Spring Rivers"

*Great Lakes Review* Narrative Map Project, "A Boy among Books"

*Hawai'i Pacific Review*, "Death of the Fugitive Charles Floyd"

*I Have My Own Song for It* (University of Akron Press), "Black River Bridge 1"

*Jenny Magazine*, "Black River Bridge 2"

*Kestrel: A Journal of Literature and Art*, "Hard Shale Dreams"

*Los Angeles Review*, "Double Exposure" and "Ferry Crossing"

*Pithead Chapel,* "Shadows of Crows Crossing Over"
*Silver Apples of the Moon,* (Cleveland State University Press), "A Brief Meditation on Color"
*Wild Roof Journal,* "Cartographer's Tale"

\* \* \*

"The Valdemar Car" was nominated by Terese Svoboda for a Pushcart Prize in Nonfiction.
*Writer Magazine* selected "Cartographer's Tale" as an [unpublished] Finalist for its "Your Turn" Contest.

\* \* \*

I would like to acknowledge Prosper Montagné (*Larousse Gastromonique: The Encyclopedia of Food, Wine & Cookery*) and Sherry Newman Spenzer (*Lake Shore Cemetery of Avon Lake*), whose books I used for reference.

My appreciation to Research and Graduate Studies at Kent State University for a Creative Activity Grant that provided the time for writing several of the creative nonfictions included in this collection. My sincere gratitude to Vermont Studio Center for awarding me the Ohio Arts Council Writing Fellowship that provided the time and space for completing the first draft of this manuscript.

I am indebted to the friends, editors, and others whose inspiration or support of my writing made this book of creative nonfiction possible: Molly Fuller, Shannon and Brian Young, Matthew Mackey, Bob Kunzinger, Kristen Lillvis, Ann Beeman, Chila Woychik, Kimberly Crum and Bonnie Omer Johnson, Donna Long, Ander Monson, Terese Svoboda, Barbara Sabol, Richard Hague, Angela Sorby, David Giffels, and Morgan Dyer, whose artwork is featured on the cover of this book (see more of her work at morgandyer.com).

My sincere appreciation to Ross K. Tangedal, Director & Publisher of Cornerstone Press, who believed in the merits of this book and has been an excellent shepherd and patient manager of this project. Working with a teaching press wherein students are fully engaged in the process has been an enriching and valued experience. Thanks to all the talented members of the student staff, especially to Gavrielle McClug, Abigail Shortell, Shelby Ballweg, Colton Bahr, and editor-in-chief Colin Aspinall, who is as fine an editor as I have had the pleasure to work with.

ROBERT MILTNER is the author of two books of prose poetry, *Hotel Utopia* and *Orpheus & Echo*, poetry chapbooks including *Against the Simple, Queen Mab and the Moon Boy, Imperative*, and *Eurydice Rising*, and the short story collection *And Your Bird Can Sing*. He has co-edited three scholarly collections of critical essays, and is the founding editor of *The Raymond Carver Review*.

Miltner is the recipient of an Ohio Arts Council Individual Excellence Award for Poetry, an Ohio Arts Council Fellowship at Vermont Studio Center, and a writing residency at Wassaic Project. His writing has received a Wick Chapbook Award from Kent State University, a Many Voices Project in Poetry Award from New Rivers Press, and a Summer Chapbook Award from Red Berry Fine Press Editions, and he has been a finalist for the National Poetry Series, the Louise Bogan Award for Artistic Merit and Excellence, the New York Center for the Book chapbook prize, and the Ohioana Award in Poetry. He has been nominated for both a Pushcart Prize and a Best of the Net Award.

A professor emeritus of English at Kent State University Stark and the NEOMFA in Creative Writing, Miltner lives in Northeast Ohio with his wife, the writer Molly Fuller.